the world of the Medieval
KNIGHT

Christopher Gravett

★

Illustrations by
Brett Breckon

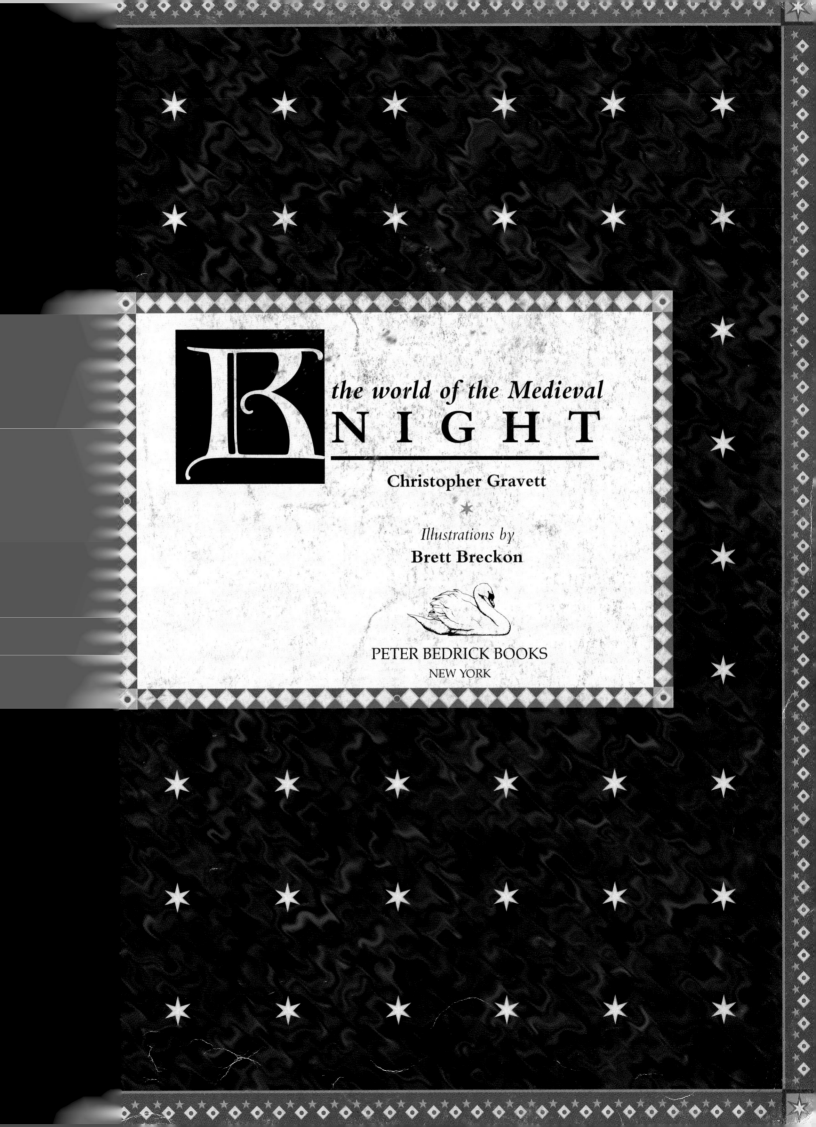

PETER BEDRICK BOOKS
NEW YORK

Author's dedication
For Jane and Joanna

Artist's dedication
For Billy and Louis

Published in 1996 by
PETER BEDRICK BOOKS
2112 Broadway
New York, N.Y. 10023

Text © Macdonald Young Books 1996
Illustration © Brett Breckon 1996

Design: Olwen Fowler
Commissioning editor: Debbie Fox
Text editor: Molly Perham

Special thanks to
Ian Eaves, formerly Keeper of Armour
at The Royal Armouries, Karen Watts
and Chris Dobson, resident armorer
at The Royal Armouries

Library of Congress
Cataloging-in-Publication Data
Gravett, Christopher, 1951–
The world of the Medieval Knight /
Christopher Gravett :
illustrations by Brett Breckon.
p.   cm.
Includes index.
ISBN 0-87226-277-4
1. Knights and knighthood—Europe—
History.   2. Knights and knighthood—
Europe—History—Pictorial works.
I. Title.
OR4513.G73   1996
940.1—dc20   96-32958
CIP

Printed and bound in Portugal
by Edições ASA
First edition, 1996
Second Printing, 1997

CHRISTOPHER GRAVETT

Christopher Gravett obtained a Masters degree in
Medieval Studies from the University of London.
He was a Curator in the British Museum before
moving to the Royal Armouries in the Tower
of London. He has written a number of articles
about the medieval era as well as several books
for adults and children.

BRETT BRECKON

Brett Breckon studied art and design in Shrewsbury
then Newport, where he gained his degree. Since
graduating, he has worked from his base in Wales as
a freelance illustrator for advertising companies and
publishing houses. An award-winning artist, he is
also the author of a book about airbrush illustration.
The World of the Medieval Knight brought him the
opportunity to delve deeply into an area of personal
interest and became his largest project to date.

CONTENTS

7 ..... Introduction

8 ..... The castle

10 ..... Castle life

12 ..... Manors and towns

14 ..... Training a knight

16 ..... Armor

18 ..... Leg defenses

20 ..... The cuirass

22 ..... Arm defenses

24 ..... Gauntlets

26 ..... Helmets

28 ..... Arming a knight

30 ..... Weapons

32 ..... Making armor

34 ..... Horses

36 ..... Retainers

38 ..... Siege warfare

40 ..... Battle

42 ..... Tournament

44 ..... Jousting

46 ..... Foot combat

48 ..... Crusades

50 ..... Hunting

52 ..... Food and banquets

54 ..... Chivalry

56 ..... Ladies

58 ..... Decline

60 ..... The knight's world

62 ..... Glossary

64 ..... Index

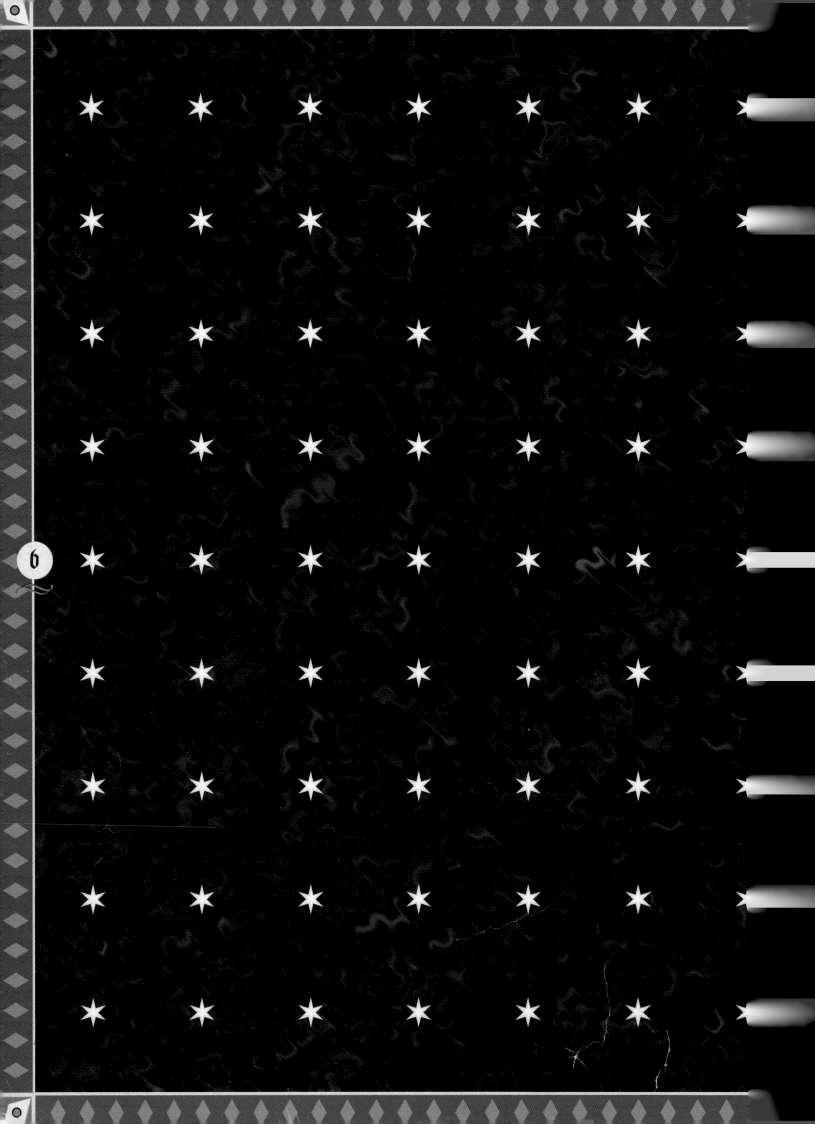

INTRODUCTION

The knight in shining armor rides a white horse and rescues maidens from dark castles. But how far is this simply the stuff of legends? When did the knight first appear? There have always been men in armor, so what makes the knight so different?

Long after the Roman Empire collapsed, the people who settled in France and Germany, called the Franks, were ruled by the great Emperor Charlemagne. When he died in AD 814 civil wars broke out, and the disruption was made worse by Viking raids from Scandinavia. People turned to the local noblemen for protection.

The nobles recruited followers to fight for them - men who were wealthy enough to own horses, as well as armor and weapons. They swore loyalty to their lord in return for land. These rough, uncultured, mounted warriors could be called the first knights. Many of them lived with their lord behind ditches topped with timber palisades, which were the first castles.

Of course, all this is very different from our ideal of the fifteenth-century knight in his shining plate armor. It took several centuries of influence from the Church, popular stories and ladies to create cultured men of manners. Being set apart by wealth and fighting skills gave knights a feeling of brotherhood, and this led to the development of orders of chivalry.

Not all early knights were rough and crude, but then not all the knights of the fifteenth century were chivalrous and well-mannered either. There were cruel but cultured nobles; there were mercenary captains; there were men who dressed like knights but who would always remain squires or men-at-arms. The knight was a character of many parts.

This 13th-century gatehouse is protected by a drawbridge, iron-framed portcullis and thick wooden doors.

Keeps and Curtains

The first wooden castles sometimes had an earth mound, or motte, in an enclosure called a bailey. By the twelfth century stone towers, or keeps, were becoming common. These had several floors above basement storerooms, with the entrance on the first floor for safety. Timber palisades were often replaced by 'curtain' walls defended by towers and a gatehouse.

THE CASTLE

A medieval knight sometimes lived in a castle surrounded by a wooden fence called a palisade, or walls, and a ditch. These fortifications provided protection against enemy attack. From his fortress a knight controlled and defended the countryside for miles around. But the castle was also the knight's home, where he lived with his family and household servants, and his garrison – the men who defended it. Castles were usually built near a river, or other water supply, and ideally on a hill or on steep rocks that were difficult to attack. They often overlooked a mountain pass or a river crossing, where the garrison could stop an enemy advancing or cut off their supplies. A line of castles sited in this way could defend a whole frontier.

Arrow 'loops' in the walls were narrow on the outside to protect the archers, but widened out inside to provide a greater firing area.

The keep, a stone tower at the center of the castle, was known in medieval times as a donjon.

Mural Towers

The outer walls were often strengthened with projecting 'mural' towers from which the defenders could shoot sideways at enemies who tried to climb the walls or dig out stones from the bottom. Each of these towers cut off a section of the wall, making it more difficult for an enemy to pass from section to section of the castle.

Archers on the high inner wall of a concentric castle could shoot arrows over the outer wall.

Round Towers

The sharp corners of square towers were a weak spot for the enemy's battering rams. They were also difficult for archers to see around. By the thirteenth century circular keeps and towers had developed as an answer to the problem.

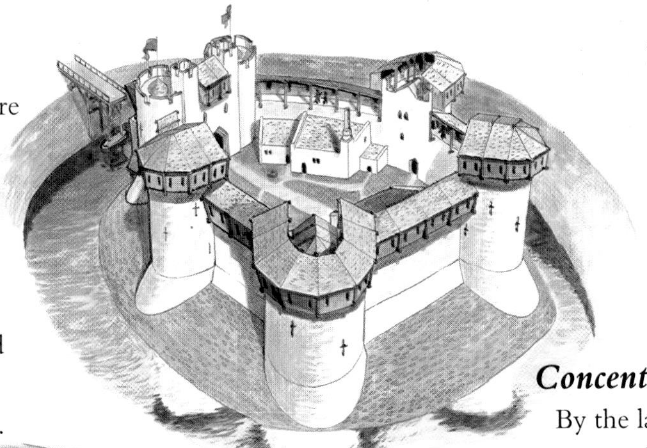

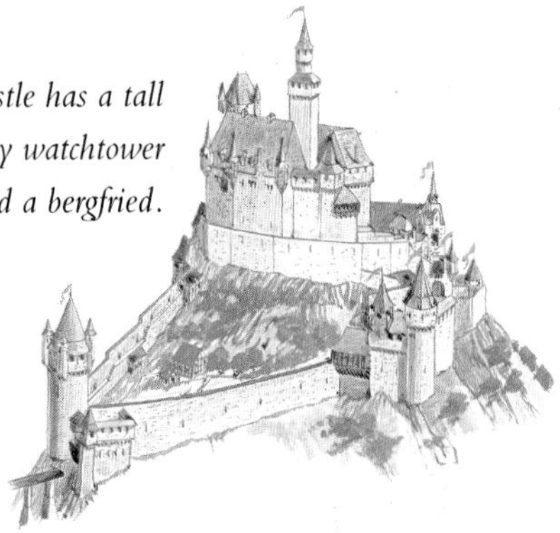

This German castle has a tall 12th-century watchtower called a bergfried.

Concentric Castles

By the late thirteenth century, many castles were built with additional courtyards for the storerooms, workshops, and stables, all protected by walls. Concentric castles had two rings of walls: these were either erected at the same time, or a second wall was added around an existing one. Caerphilly Castle in South Wales, shown below, is an example of a concentric castle. It also has huge gatehouses and a dam. Caerphilly Castle was built between 1268-77.

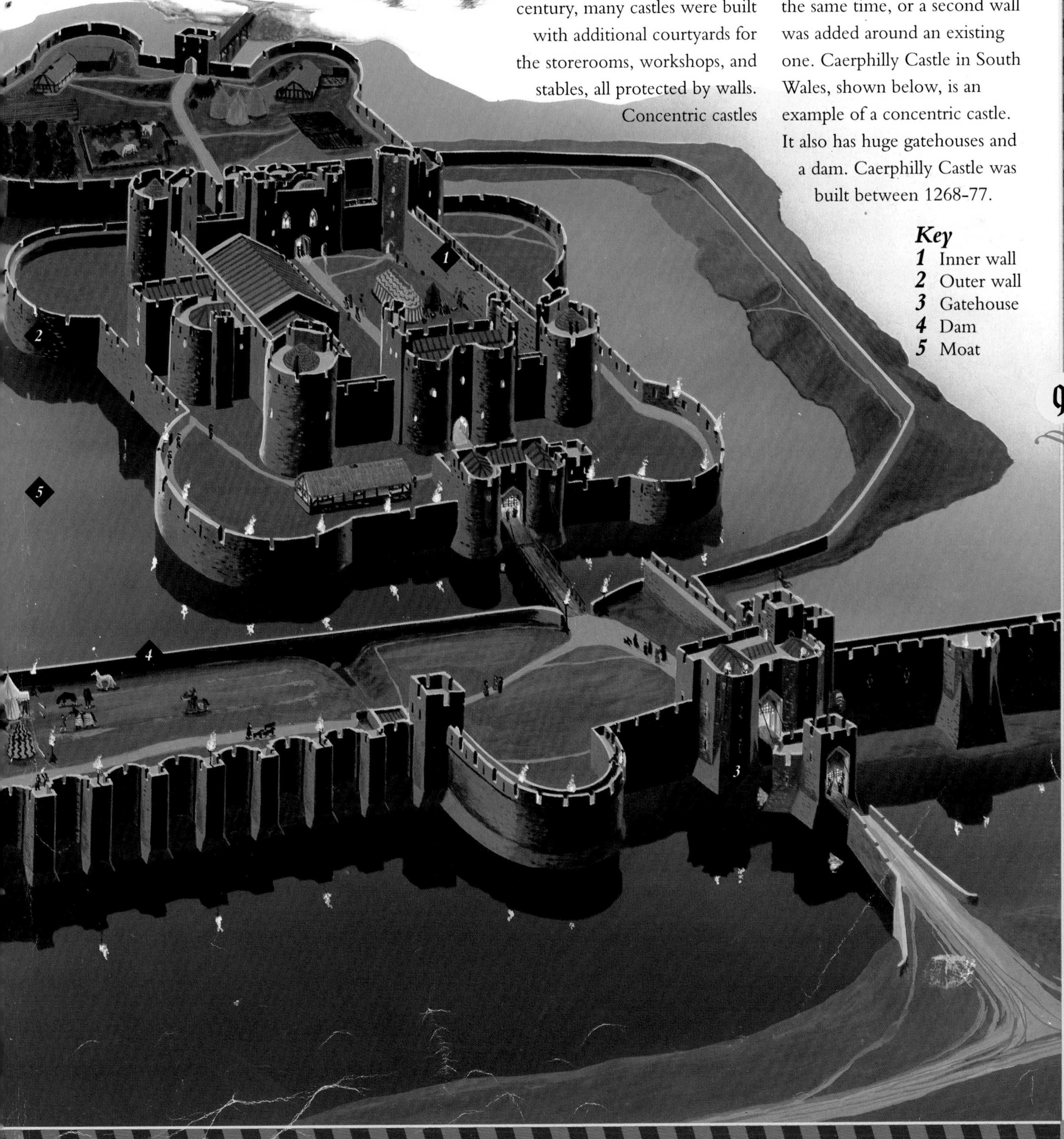

Key
1 Inner wall
2 Outer wall
3 Gatehouse
4 Dam
5 Moat

CASTLE LIFE

This illustration shows how Chepstow Castle in Monmouthshire looked in about 1285. This layout was used in many castles of this period. In earlier castles the lord usually ate, conducted business and slept in the hall with everybody else and so had very little privacy. It became more popular, however, for lords and their families to have their own private living area. There were other buildings in the castle too, including stores for food, a chapel for daily services, a smithy for shoeing horses and making things like nails and hinges, and an armorer's workshop for repairing armor and weapons. Every castle had a well in case there was ever a siege. Sometimes there was a bakehouse and a brewery and some later castles had herb gardens and flower gardens to stroll in. Many people attended great lords including a steward, marshal, sewer (head waiter and taster), butler and cup-bearer.

Not all castles had fireplaces. Some had central hearths and the smoke from the fires escaped through wooden louvres. If a castle did not have a fire, servants would build fires in portable braziers - iron containers on legs - but the rooms would often get very smoky! However, as soon as stone was used for building castles, fireplaces could be built in the wall with flues or chimneys to carry the smoke away. The fireplaces were often beautifully decorated.

10

Key

1 Gatehouse, incorporating guardroom
2 Defensive hoarding
3 Prison
4 Barbican
5 Private chambers (inside)
6 Guardroom (inside)
7 Kitchen
8 Open hearth
9 Ventilation turret
10 External staircase from kitchen to chambers
11 Service passage
12 Latrines
13 Cellar
14 Boat bringing supplies
15+16 Pantries for dry food
17 Pantry for bottles
18 Private chamber
19 Great Hall
20 High table

Inside the Castle

The Great Hall was the central part of life in a castle. Here you can see cooks and servants preparing food and serving it. The hall is plastered, painted and hung with tapestries to add color. At one end there is a decorative wooden screen which guards against the cold drafts from the doors. Large carved windows sometimes had glass instead of shutters, but were more expensive. You can see that the kitchen is connected to the hall

by a staircase so that food could be served quickly before going cold. In some castles the kitchen buildings were separate to reduce the risk of fire. A winch has been set up in the cellar for food supplies coming in by boats moored on the rocks below.

Because this castle was built next to a river, its lavatories were built over the edge of the cliff and the waste was simply washed away.

The prison was in the basement and this was used for prisoners awaiting trial. Prisoners of high rank were usually well looked after because the lord would receive a high ransom for them.

Sentries kept watch from the battlements, part of their 'castle-guard' duty for their lord. Sometimes hired guards would be used instead.

Aerial View

MANORS AND TOWNS

Many knights held land from rich nobles, or from the king, in return for service. The amount of land varied enormously, from a small village to great tracts of countryside. A knight was lord of the manor on his estate. The manor house was the grandest building. Beyond were the houses and huts of the villagers, as well as the church and the mill for grinding corn. The knight had many rights over the villagers, but in return he owed them his protection and at certain festivals, such as harvest-time, he fed them at his expense. The villagers were of all ranks. In the eleventh century there were slaves in England who had no rights. Slavery gradually disappeared, but huge numbers of peasants were unfree and belonged to the lord. The Black Death, the bubonic plague which struck Europe in 1348, killed so many people that workers became valuable and this, together with increased wealth, meant that there were many more farmers who were free, rather than being tied to a particular lord.

Peasants often paid dues to their lord with farm produce rather than money. Here a squire is receiving the eggs on behalf of his lord. Those who managed to produce more than they or the lord needed could sell them to earn some money.

12

A Village
This picture shows an imaginary medieval village. Villages varied enormously, depending on the type of landscape and climate.

In fairly open areas, two or three huge fields were worked by the villagers who owned strips of land in them. In hilly parts of England, villagers often raised sheep for wool, whereas in the warmer areas of Europe, vines were grown to produce grapes for wine. Woods and forests were owned by the lord so that he could go hunting.

Only charcoal burners were allowed to burn wood to make charcoal.

Fields
These fields are divided into strips for each family in the village. Villagers also had to work on the lord's home farm.

Tithe Barn
The church took a 'tithe', or tenth, of all produce, and this was stored in a large wooden barn.

Stocks
The lord held 'manor courts' and justice was carried out there and then. Here wrongdoers are locked in the stocks and pelted with old food by the villagers.

Poachers
Men who poached deer or other animals on the lord's land faced severe penalties if they were caught, from fines to the loss of a hand or foot.

Towns

Merchants flocked to the towns to buy and sell produce – spices from the East, furs from Russia and amber from the Baltic. Many towns bought a charter from the king, which gave them the freedom to conduct their own affairs. In the town pictured here, the streets are crowded with wooden houses and shops, and fires are frequent. The upper stories of the houses stick out, making the streets dark. A knight might buy a town house because it was convenient for trading in the market, and for when the knight had to perform castle-guard – his duties in the noble's castle. Some knights had to attend the courts, or even parliament, as knights of the shire. Many Spanish knights lived within walled towns, for Spain was constantly at war against the Moors, Muslims from North Africa.

The Manor House

A lord held feasts at his manor house and also held court. Some very grand manor houses were built in the 15th century.

Church

The church was the center of religious life. It was also used for public events. Couples were betrothed at the door in a ceremony almost as binding as the wedding.

Water Mill

Peasants had to grind their corn at the lord's mill and pay for it. Millers had a bad reputation for adding sand to flour to make up the weight.

Cows and Horses in the Water Meadow

Cattle and horses were allowed to graze the grass in the water meadow.

Bread Ovens

Villagers were expected to bake their bread in the lord's ovens and they paid for the privilege!

Pigs in the Wood

Pigs were allowed in the lord's woodland in autumn to root for acorns and beechmast.

RAINING A KNIGHT

After some lessons at home young boys were often sent to a lord's castle to be trained for knighthood, sometimes even when they were only seven years old. The young trainee knight was known as a page. He ran errands and began to learn about horses, armor and weapons. When he was about fourteen he became a squire and was apprenticed to a knight.

A young page learned courtesy and grace while waiting on a lady. Sometimes he would play chess or checkers with the lady, or sing or play instruments. Some pages might even be taught to read and write by a priest, a clerk or an educated lady.

The Hunting Field

Because hunting was so popular, pages and squires had to learn how to handle falcons and hawks. They also had to be able to 'break', or cut up, a deer.

A page or squire practiced against a wooden stake, or 'pell', to develop muscles and skill. He also practiced against other squires and learned to shoot, not for war, but for hunting.

Pages and squires were expected to serve at the table in front of the knights and were taught how to carve the meat properly. They had to develop these skills before they could be knighted.

Squires had to follow their master on the battlefield to protect him if he fell. From the 13th century, squires sometimes fought beside him.

Training for Battle

A page or squire had to get so used to armor that wearing it became second nature. He had to practice with a lance so that it did not run back through his fingers when he struck the knight. If he hit the swinging quintain he had to ride quickly past or receive a buffet from the weighted bag!

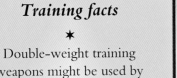

Pages cleaned rust from mail by rolling it in a barrel of sand.

Girding the Sword

When considered ready, (sometime between the ages of eighteen and twenty one), a squire was dubbed, often by the knight who trained him. He might have a symbolic bath to cleanse himself, and he would watch over his weapons and armor in the chapel all night. This was known as the vigil. The following morning, he would be dressed in symbolically colored clothes – red (for his blood), white (for purity), and brown (the return to earth on death). Gilded spurs were fastened on his ankles and he was 'girded' with a sword. He was dubbed a knight by a tap on each shoulder with a sword and reminded of the ideals he should fight for.

Training facts

★

Double-weight training weapons might be used by squires so that they would improve their muscles.

★

Originally 'dubbing' was a cuff by the hand on the neck.

★

Before the 13th century many squires found it so costly to be knighted that they tried to avoid it.

★

The King sometimes knighted a number of squires before a battle to make up the number of knights.

15

ARMOR

This early 14th-century shield is made of wood and covered with decorated leather. Carrying and hanging straps are riveted to the back.

The picture below shows how armor developed from the mail coat of interlinked iron rings on the left, to the full plate armor on the right. Mail armor was tough, but it was also flexible, so a blow from a heavy weapon could still break bones even if it did not tear the iron links. As better weapons were made, armorers designed stronger armor to withstand them. Solid plates of steel, or even hardened leather, became increasingly popular to protect against swords with sharp points and narrow, needle-like arrowheads. Full plate armor had strong plates with smooth, curved surfaces to make weapon points skid off. Yet it was still light enough to be worn easily. Very rich men ordered their armor from one of the famous workshops in Germany or Italy. They sent their measurements, or items of clothing, to make sure the armor fitted perfectly.

Less well-off knights probably bought 'off the peg' from local armorers, who had stocks of ready-made pieces.

The Age of Mail

This eleventh-century knight wears a hauberk, a mail coat of interlinked iron rings. The skirt is split at the front and back for riding. A mail coat weighed about 30 pounds, and the weight tended to make it drag from the shoulders and arms. The large wooden shield guards the knight's left side and part of his horse's flank when he is mounted. The conical helmet has a noseguard to protect the knight's nose against slashing cuts from an enemy's sword.

16

From Mail to Plate

The thirteenth-century knight (second from the left) has mail on his hands, legs and feet. The colorful outer garment, called a surcoat, may have provided protection from the rain or heat – or may simply have been copied from Muslim dress. The knight is carrying his great helm, which has a chain for slinging over the shoulder. The shield is smaller than that of the eleventh-century knight. The knight of about 1350 (third from left) has a coat of plates over the mail and gutter-shaped plates on his arms and legs. He is wearing a basinet rather than a great helm. By 1400 some knights wore armor made almost entirely of uncovered steel plates. Shields were hardly needed and often used only in tournaments.

The knight on the right is how the Earl of Warwick, a powerful knight who was killed in 1471, may have looked. Plate armor could be shaped, so it followed fashion. Armor-making centers produced their own styles – this English armor is mainly Italian in style, with some features that were used on German armors. The Earl is mounting his horse without any assistance. This is because his armor weighed only 45-55 pounds, less than a modern infantryman carries on his back, and the weight was spread all over his body. The knight could run, lie down, or even turn cartwheels while wearing full armor. Some knights boasted of vaulting into the saddle, or climbing up the underside of a scaling ladder. A knight wore underwear beneath his armor, and could untie two laces under his mail skirt when he wanted to relieve himself. However, the armor got extremely hot inside because body heat could not escape. Knights who got trapped in a crush of men often suffocated.

Mail stockings, or chausses, had a lace threaded through below the knee to prevent them sagging. No one is quite sure exactly how chausses were tied at the top, but this is a likely method of keeping them up.

Leg Armor facts

★

Surviving greaves show that many knights had very slim calves. Nobody is quite sure why this is so, but it is possibly the result of riding much more often than walking.

★

Skeletons in war graves from a battle in Gotland, Sweden, in 1361 show that leg wounds were the most common, though how many wore leg armor or rode horses is not known.

★

At the Siege of Orleans in 1429, Joan of Arc trod on a caltrop, a small spiked weapon, which pierced the leather sole of her foot armor.

L E G   D E F E N S E S

When a knight was mounted on his horse, his legs made a good target for foot soldiers. Knights rarely wore leg armor until the twelfth century, when some of them began to lace a strip of mail over the front of their legs. Others wore stockings made of mail, with a leather sole to make walking easier. A blow to the kneecap could cripple a knight for life, so when plate leg defenses were introduced in the thirteenth century, the knee was often the first area to be protected, by a cup-shaped poleyn. By the late fourteenth century, most of the leg and foot was covered in plates. The plates that protected the shin and calf, which were shaped to fit over even the ankle bones, were some of the most difficult to make. Various other materials such as hardened leather, whalebone and horn were used as well as steel. In the late fourteenth century, thigh defenses, or cuisses, were often studded with rivets, which held small metal plates underneath. They were made like the coat called the brigandine.

Late 13th-century gamboised (padded) cuisse, poleyn and schynbald (shin-defense)

Late 14th-century greave of leather with steel strips riveted on

Late 14th-century leg-defense made entirely of steel plates

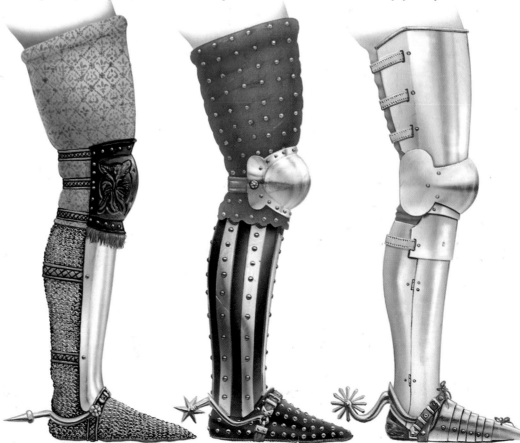

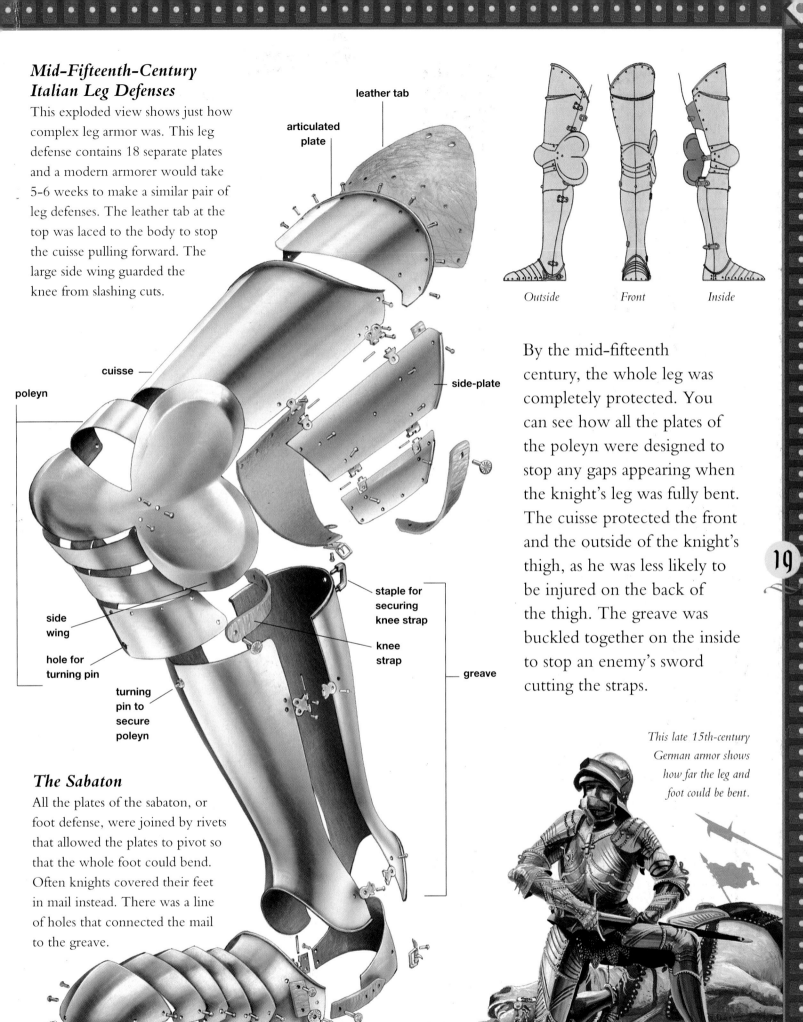

Mid-Fifteenth-Century Italian Leg Defenses

This exploded view shows just how complex leg armor was. This leg defense contains 18 separate plates and a modern armorer would take 5-6 weeks to make a similar pair of leg defenses. The leather tab at the top was laced to the body to stop the cuisse pulling forward. The large side wing guarded the knee from slashing cuts.

leather tab

articulated plate

cuisse

poleyn

side-plate

side wing

hole for turning pin

turning pin to secure poleyn

staple for securing knee strap

knee strap

greave

Outside   *Front*   *Inside*

By the mid-fifteenth century, the whole leg was completely protected. You can see how all the plates of the poleyn were designed to stop any gaps appearing when the knight's leg was fully bent. The cuisse protected the front and the outside of the knight's thigh, as he was less likely to be injured on the back of the thigh. The greave was buckled together on the inside to stop an enemy's sword cutting the straps.

19

The Sabaton

All the plates of the sabaton, or foot defense, were joined by rivets that allowed the plates to pivot so that the whole foot could bend. Often knights covered their feet in mail instead. There was a line of holes that connected the mail to the greave.

This late 15th-century German armor shows how far the leg and foot could be bent.

sabaton

This padded tunic, called an aketon, was also worn under mail to absorb blows. It had a solid collar.

THE CUIRASS

Armor for the main part of the body is called the cuirass. Its name comes from a French word for leather, 'cuir'. Until the fourteenth century most knights wore a mail coat called a 'hauberk', usually with a padded tunic underneath to absorb blows. Some wore a coat of scales. By the early thirteenth century some knights added a defense of hardened leather to help protect their chest and back. This was the 'curie' and it was laced or buckled together at the side and worn over the mail but under the surcoat. Some knights lined the front of their surcoat with plates. By about 1300 the popular coat of plates appeared, which had a lining of metal plates. Then a solid breastplate developed. By 1400 all the plates were usually worn uncovered, connected by rivets or internal straps. This was known as 'alwite' (all white) armor.

This coat had separate scales riveted to a canvas backing.

Iron or steel plates were riveted to the inside of the canvas. The rivet heads can be seen on the outside. They were sometimes shaped like flowers.

The Coat of Plates
This coat of plates from the mid-fourteenth century has shoulder-guards. It was put on over the knight's head, then buckled and laced behind. Beautiful rich fabrics were often used. Edward III used cloth of gold, velvet and white leather.

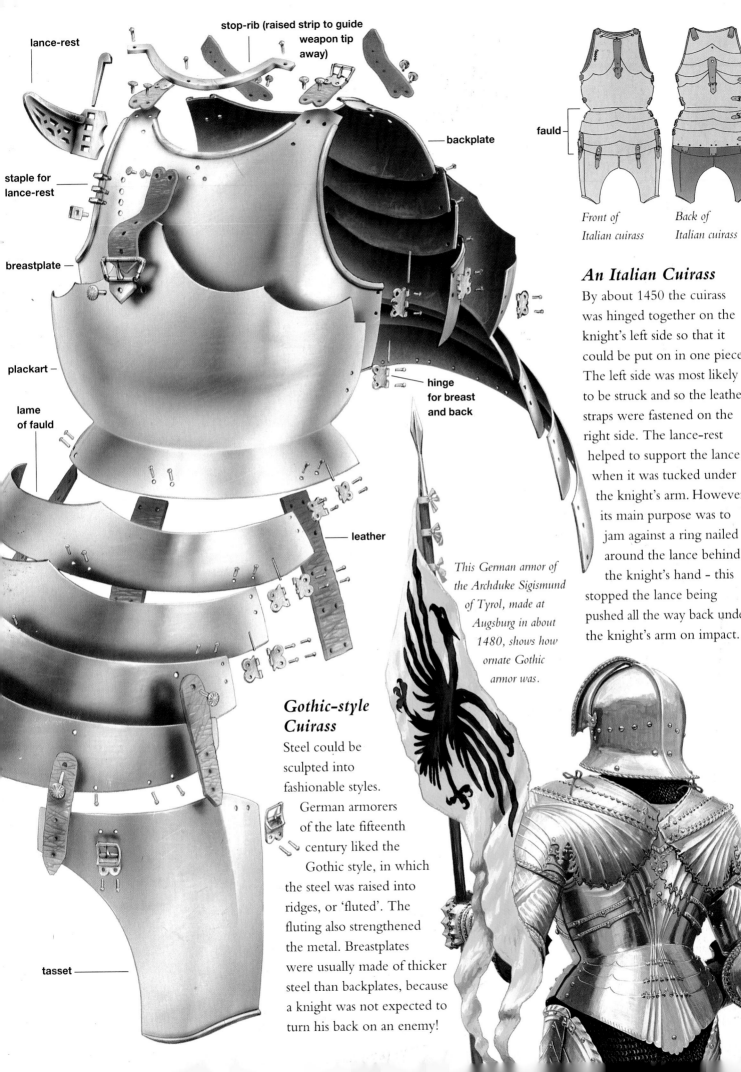

lance-rest

stop-rib (raised strip to guide weapon tip away)

backplate

staple for lance-rest

breastplate —

plackart —

lame of fauld

hinge for breast and back

leather

tasset —

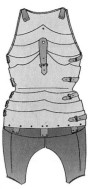

fauld

Front of Italian cuirass

Back of Italian cuirass

An Italian Cuirass

By about 1450 the cuirass was hinged together on the knight's left side so that it could be put on in one piece. The left side was most likely to be struck and so the leather straps were fastened on the right side. The lance-rest helped to support the lance when it was tucked under the knight's arm. However, its main purpose was to jam against a ring nailed around the lance behind the knight's hand – this stopped the lance being pushed all the way back under the knight's arm on impact.

This German armor of the Archduke Sigismund of Tyrol, made at Augsburg in about 1480, shows how ornate Gothic armor was.

Gothic-style Cuirass

Steel could be sculpted into fashionable styles. German armorers of the late fifteenth century liked the Gothic style, in which the steel was raised into ridges, or 'fluted'. The fluting also strengthened the metal. Breastplates were usually made of thicker steel than backplates, because a knight was not expected to turn his back on an enemy!

ARM DEFENSES

This painting of Sir Hugh Hastings in about 1340 is based on a picture on his tomb. He wears gutter-shaped plates on the outside of his arms, cups called elbow-cops on his elbows, and discs laced on at his elbow and shoulder.

The knight's shoulders were a main target for his opponent, and they were especially vulnerable to sword blows that skidded off the helmet. The arms were more difficult to hit because the left arm was protected by a shield, and the right arm was constantly moving as the knight wielded his weapon. All the same, a broken arm or elbow would disable a knight in combat, and did not always heal properly, which could wreck his career. Early knights protected their arms with mail sleeves that reached to the elbow. By the twelfth century they came down to the wrist. It seems that solid plates were not used until about 1300, beginning with plates on the outside of the arm and simple discs at the shoulder and elbow. This protection for the whole arm was called a vambrace. By 1350 the knight's arms were completely protected and even the elbow defense developed a 'wing', which helped protect the elbow from sharp weapons.

Some 14th-century knights, especially Germans, wore what appears to be leather reinforced by metal strips.

The Three-Part Vambrace
Some fifteenth-century German knights preferred an older style of three-piece arm defense. Here the squire is about to lace and buckle on the cup-shaped plate for the elbow, called a couter. The upper cannon has already been laced to the upper arm and the lower cannon slid over the forearm.

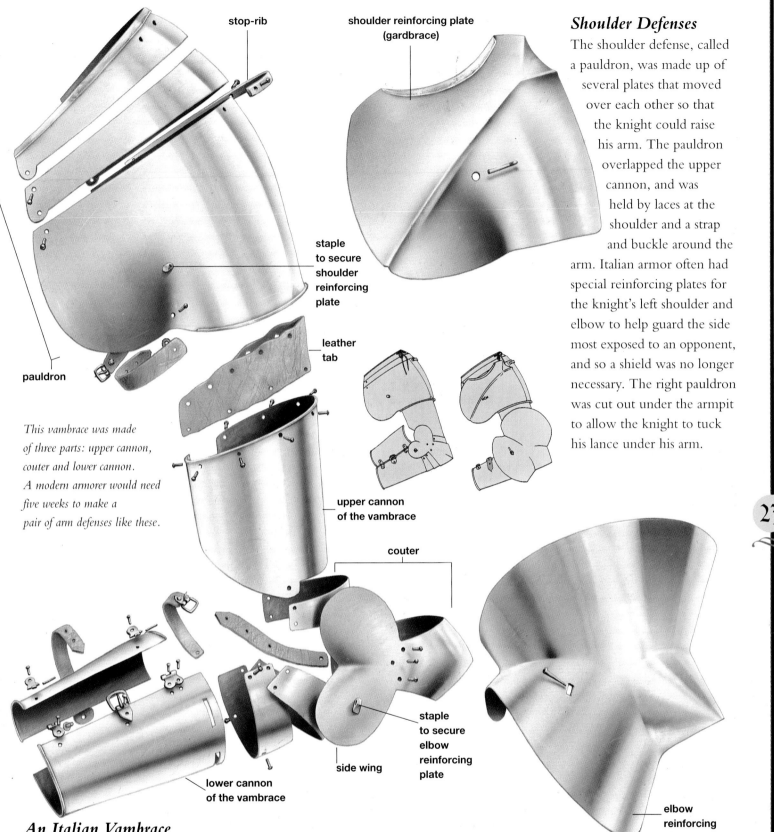

stop-rib

shoulder reinforcing plate
(gardbrace)

pauldron

staple
to secure
shoulder
reinforcing
plate

leather
tab

*This vambrace was made
of three parts: upper cannon,
couter and lower cannon.
A modern armorer would need
five weeks to make a
pair of arm defenses like these.*

upper cannon
of the vambrace

couter

lower cannon
of the vambrace

side wing

staple
to secure
elbow
reinforcing
plate

elbow
reinforcing
plate
(guard
of the
vambrace)

Shoulder Defenses

The shoulder defense, called a pauldron, was made up of several plates that moved over each other so that the knight could raise his arm. The pauldron overlapped the upper cannon, and was held by laces at the shoulder and a strap and buckle around the arm. Italian armor often had special reinforcing plates for the knight's left shoulder and elbow to help guard the side most exposed to an opponent, and so a shield was no longer necessary. The right pauldron was cut out under the armpit to allow the knight to tuck his lance under his arm.

23

An Italian Vambrace

This mid-fifteenth-century vambrace was fastened to the shoulder by laces tied through holes in the leather tab at the top of the upper cannon. The hinged plates of the lower cannon were closed around the knight's forearm and held in place by a strap and buckle. The small plates above and below the couter stopped any gaps appearing when the knight bent his arms. The lowest plate was attached to the lower cannon by rivets, each sliding in a slot cut in the upper end of the cannon, so that the knight could twist his forearm. The pictures on the right each show (left) a sliding rivet and (right) how two plates pivot on a single rivet.

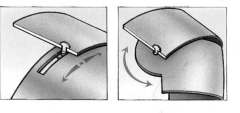

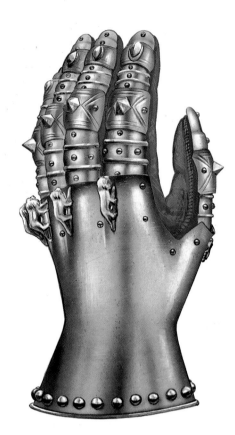

AUNTLETS

The first knights did not wear any armor on their hands. They relied on their shield and the sword's cross-guard, a metal bar in front of the hand, to protect them. In about 1180 knights started to defend their hands by extending the sleeves of their mailcoats to form 'mufflers' or mittens. This was popular for about 150 years. Towards the end of the thirteenth century some knights started to wear a separate, rather baggy glove or gauntlet, probably made of leather. From this came a gauntlet that had scales of whalebone or metal attached to cloth, or riveted between two layers of material, with the rivet heads showing on the surface. By about 1350 most knights wore their gauntlets with the plates on the outside. They had separate fingers, each protected by a row of small plates. By 1430 gauntlets shaped like steel mittens had taken over, but separate fingers re-appeared in certain areas towards the end of the fifteenth century.

The gauntlet above was made for the Black Prince, who died in 1376. It is a typical 'hour-glass' shape – the cuff neatly flares out – and the fingers have separate scales. Each knuckle is fitted with a gadling, a raised piece of metal. With these, a knight could use his clenched fist like brass knuckles. The gadlings of the Black Prince were cast in the shape of lions.

This early 14th-century gauntlet is made from scales of tough whalebone attached to a glove.

Mufflers

Most knights in the thirteenth century wore mail mufflers, which were extensions of the knight's sleeves. Their palms were covered by cloth or leather to give a better grip. The difficulty came when, as with this wounded crusader, the muffler had to be removed. To cope with this, a slit was made in the palm so that the knight could push his hand through it. A thong threaded through the mail at the wrist stopped the mail above dragging over his hand.

Gauntlet facts
★

If a knight's honor was questioned he might 'throw down the gauntlet' to challenge his accuser to combat. If the accuser picked it up, he accepted the challenge.

★

At the coronation banquet of English monarchs, the king's champion knight rode fully-armed into Westminster Hall. He threw down the gauntlet to defy anyone who challenged the new king's right to rule.

Italian Gauntlet

This exploded view shows how a mitten gauntlet was put together in about 1450. The plates fitted around a leather glove, so that putting on a gauntlet was just like putting on an armored glove. The palm was not covered in steel, so that a knight could grip his sword easily. The left gauntlet often had only one plate over the fingers, because most knights grasped their weapons with the right hand and so it didn't need to be so flexible.

They added more straps across the underside of the fingers to take the strain from the stitches.

A Steel Glove

There are 26 metal plates in this gauntlet. The glove is hand-stitched to leather or canvas lining bands riveted inside the edges of the plates. Each finger-end is protected by small 'scales' riveted to a leather strip, which is then stitched to the glove itself.

A German Gauntlet

After about 1430 German gauntlets were like mittens, but in the later fifteenth century some, like this one holding a rondel dagger, were made with completely separate fingers. This beautifully made gauntlet was made for an Archduke. Each finger joint was covered with a gadling, which overlapped the scale above and below it. The knight could make his hand into a fist without exposing any of the glove.

★

We know from the inventory made on the death of the knight Raoul de Nesle in 1302, that he paid 20 shillings (£1) for two pairs of gauntlets covered in red leather. That is roughly equivalent to $570 today.

★

One knight, Sir Nicholas Bembre, who was charged with treason in 1388 offered to defend himself. There were so many challengers that the gauntlets of challengers flew down 'like snow'.

25

HELMETS

The helmet was one of the first pieces of armor to be made from solid plate. One of the earliest types in many parts of Europe was the conical helmet. This was fitted with a nasal, or nose-guard, to protect against slashing swords. By the end of the twelfth century some helmets had face-guards, and soon the whole head was enclosed in a great helm, with vision slits and holes to allow the knight to breathe. A padded arming cap underneath the helmet helped to absorb shock from heavy blows.

Many infantrymen wore the open-faced kettle hat, and even a few knights preferred it, because it allowed more air to get to their faces. The helm was hot and stuffy, and muffled hearing. By the fourteenth century some knights found the great helm too restricting and changed to lighter basinets, which often had visors and mail neck-guards.

This conical helmet was made from four plates plus a rim.

The padded arming cap was designed to absorb blows.

This great helm of the 13th century has a wood and leather crest and cloth round the top called mantling. It was sometimes worn over a steel cap.

The 13th-century cervellière was a steel cap worn over or under a mail hood.

This late 14th-century basinet had a removable visor and mail neck-guard, or aventail, to protect the neck. This was attached by a cord to staples on the helmet. When the aventail needed to be cleaned or repaired, they could remove it by pulling the cord.

The kettle hat had a wide brim that was useful for deflecting missiles dropped from above.

Cheek-piece open · Cheek-piece closed · With visor · With wrapper

Once in place, the cheek-pieces of the armet were closed and fastened. The visor dropped down over the cheek-pieces and the wrapper was fastened on last.

crest-holder

skull

padded lining

rondel

staple

cheek-piece

lining-band

visor

brow-reinforce

An Italian Armet

Here is an exploded view of a mid-fifteenth century armet, which developed from the basinet. Like all helmets, the armet had a lining of canvas stuffed with tow or hay. This lining was stitched to a canvas or leather strip and to change it, they just needed to cut the stitches. It was also possible to adjust the lining so that the knight's eyes were always in line with the vision slits. The crest-holder on top was for a wooden or leather crest. The front of the helmet was protected by a 'wrapper', and at the rear was a rondel. No one knows for certain what this was for – perhaps it stopped the wrapper strap from sliding about or helped to protect it.

The knight's chin might be protected, as here, by a 'bevor' (from the French 'to dribble'). This late 15th-century sallet is West European. Another type was very popular in Germany.

27

Helmet facts

✴

At the Battle of Hastings in 1066, Duke William of Normandy had to push back his helmet so that his men could see that he was still alive.

✴

In the twelfth century, William Marshal was found after a tournament with his head on an anvil while a smith tried to remove his battered helmet

✴

Some basinets were decorated with a jeweled cloth band called an orle.

ARMING A KNIGHT

A knight was armed by one or more squires or pages. He was always armed from the feet upwards. First the knight put on a linen shirt and drawers, which were rather like loose boxer shorts. Over the drawers he pulled on woolen hose - long stockings that were joined together at the top. You can see where the squire has bandaged his knees to stop the steel plates rubbing. When the knight was not in armor, he fastened his hose to a cloth jacket, or doublet, with points, which were laces fitted with metal tips to prevent the ends fraying. But under his armor he wore a special arming doublet, and tied, or 'pointed' his hose to this instead. The hose had a flap across the front that the knight could untie when he needed to go to the lavatory.

The arming doublet had waxed laces to attach items of armor. Patches, or gussets, of mail protected the armpit and elbow. The knight protected his neck with a mail standard, a stiff collar made from thicker rings of mail. Mail pants (center) or a mail skirt (below) were put on after the leg pieces.

Here you can see a squire attaching the poleyn and cuisse in one piece over the knee and the thigh. The poleyn locked over a stud on the greave and the cuisse was probably laced to the doublet.

28

Arming facts

✶

Sometimes a knight's armor had identifying marks stamped into it. One was the armorer's trade mark, and another was the mark of the town where the armor was made, to show that it had been passed as up to standard.

✶

In 1466 an Italian armorer visited King Louis XI to measure him for armor. He had to study the king day and night so that the armor would fit exactly.

✶

In 1441 a ready-made suit of armor from Milan cost £8 6 shillings and 14 pence.

The squire slipped on the breast and back plates and he strapped them together from the right side. On the left side they were hinged. The fauld, or skirt, is already attached. The knight could adjust the fit of the tassets, which are already buckled to his fauld.

Cap-a-pie

A knight in full armor was said to be armed cap-a-pie, an old French phrase meaning 'head to foot'. By the mid-fifteenth-century there were so many pieces of armor that you would expect it to take hours to put them all on. But many of the pieces were already attached to one another, so this was not as difficult as it looked. In fact a knight could be completely armed by two squires in ten to fifteen minutes. The last piece of armor put on was the helmet. The squire closed the armet around the knight's head and strapped the wrapper around the lower half. The helmet was very hot to wear, so if the knight was not going into action immediately, he kept his helmet to one side, and hung his gauntlets on his sword hilt.

The squire laced the arm defense through the lower pair of points. He tied on the pauldron with the upper pair of points and strapped it around the upper arm. When the pauldrons were tied and buckled in place, the squire fastened the knight's spurs to his heels. The knight did not wear spurs when fighting on foot, because they could easily trip him up.

cross-guard
tang
fuller

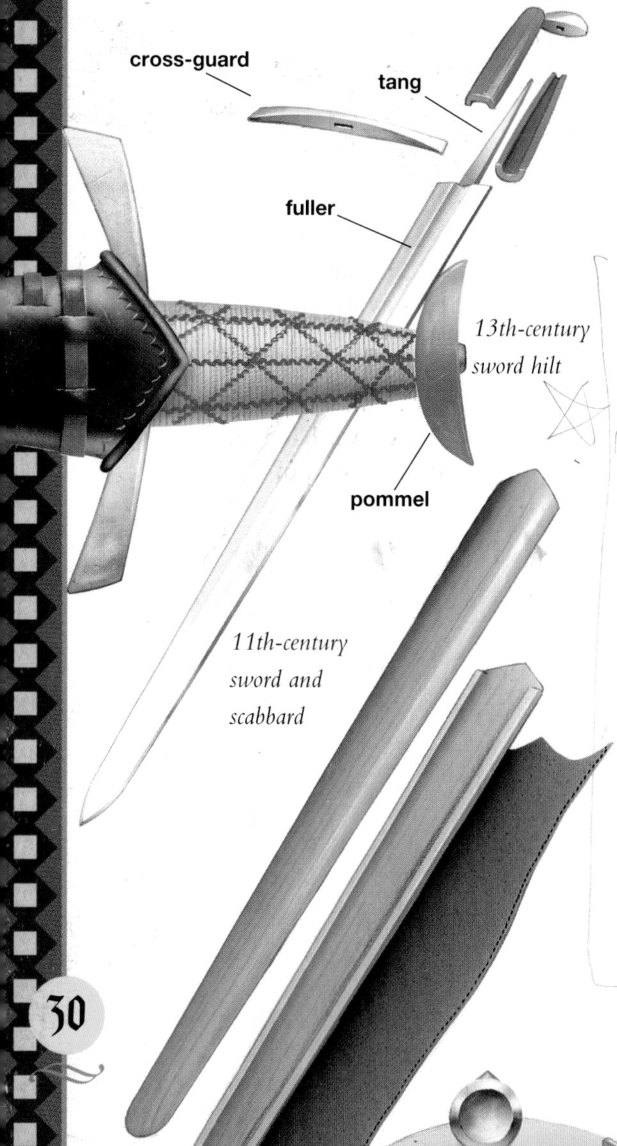

13th-century sword hilt

pommel

11th-century sword and scabbard

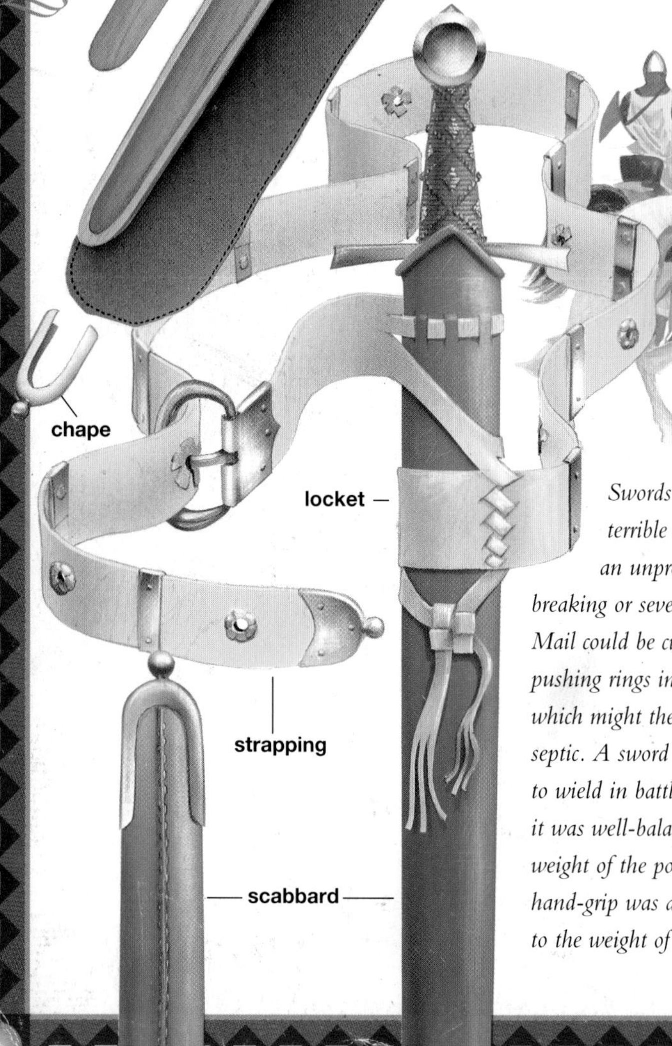

WEAPONS

A knight's chief weapon was his sword. The knights in the picture below are wielding double-edged slashing swords, but by the end of the thirteenth century swords were more pointed and the section of the blade was diamond-shaped rather than flat. This stronger, stiffer weapon could thrust through rings of mail armor. Also by this time some swords were longer – so long that knights had to use two hands to wield them. These were known as 'hand-and-a-half', or 'bastard', swords and they were hung from the horse's saddle. Some warriors used a heavy-bladed weapon like a butcher's cleaver, called a falchion. The knight's other main weapon was the lance, which had a shaft made of ash and a sharp steel point. In the eleventh century the lance was thrown like a javelin, or used for thrusting. But by about 1100 knights rode at the enemy in close formation with their lances tucked tightly under their arms. In about 1300 the vamplate, a steel disc to guard the hand, was added to the lance.

chape

locket

strapping

scabbard

Swords could inflict terrible wounds to an unprotected body, breaking or severing limbs. Mail could be cut open, pushing rings into a wound which might then become septic. A sword was easy to wield in battle because it was well-balanced. The weight of the pommel and hand-grip was almost equal to the weight of the blade.

Swords and Scabbards

Down the center of a cutting sword there was a groove called a fuller, which helped to lighten the blade. At the top the tang was covered by a wooden grip, usually bound by silk, leather or wire to stop it slipping in a sweaty hand. The pommel at the end stopped the knight's hand sliding off, and the cross-guard gave some protection against cuts from an opponent's weapon. Wooden scabbards were often covered in leather. A metal chape guarded the bottom and sometimes a metal locket was fixed at the top. The strapping on the early fourteenth-century scabbard on the left allowed it to hang at a convenient angle.

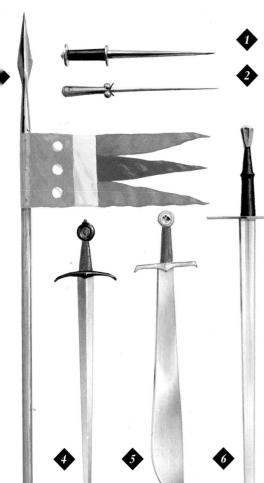

Daggers, Maces and Staff Weapons

Knights used other weapons besides swords and lances which were capable of producing horrific injuries. Axes were popular in northern Europe. By the thirteenth century some knights carried short-handled axes to use while on horseback, and daggers became more common. As the wearing of plate armor increased, knights used steel-headed maces, and later war hammers to deal crushing blows. For very heavy blows, knights used staff weapons (steel heads mounted on long wooden staffs). They were popular with infantry and sometimes with knights on foot. The pollaxe (from 'poll', meaning 'head'), had an axehead backed by a hammer or a beak. Some foot soldiers adapted agricultural tools to make staff weapons. The halberd, used by the foot soldier on the left, was popular with the Swiss and Germans. It was originally made from the blade of a plow.

Key

1. 14th-century rondel dagger
2. 15th-century ballock dagger
3. 11th-century lance
4. 14th-century thrusting sword
5. 13th-century falchion
6. 14th-century hand-and-a-half-sword
7. 14th-century horseman's axe
8. 14th-century mace
9. 15th-century war hammer
10. Late 15th-century pollaxe

Weapon facts

★

It is claimed that the long-handled axe used by the Anglo-Danes in the 11th century could cut through a horse and rider at one blow.

★

A knight's sword weighed about 2 ½ pounds.

★

Plate armor gave good protection, so daggers were thrust through mailed armpits or the vision-slits of visors.

31

Mail was made from iron wire forced through holes in a board to the required thickness, then coiled round a rod and cut into rings.

The ends of each ring were flattened and pierced with tiny holes. Each ring was linked with four others and joined with a tiny rivet.

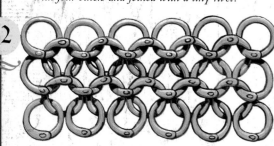

Adding or removing links of mail from a row altered the shape, rather like knitting. A coat contained thousands of rings, and weighed about 33 lbs.

Today, a modern armorer takes about four months to make a suit of armor. This busy Italian workshop could probably turn out six suits a day. After marking the steel with the shape needed for the armor, the armorer cut the sheet with huge scissor-like snips, which you can see below. The charcoal furnace on the far right heated up the steel to make it softer and easier to work. The bellows were used if more heat was needed. Next to the bellows the craftsman has been hammering a hot piece of steel over an anvil, which he has plunged into cold water to cool and, thereby, strengthen it. On the far right a helmet is being 'drawn up' over a mushroom-headed stake pushed into a hole in a tree trunk. The man at the right of the table below is doing finer shaping, while the one on the far left is fitting pieces ready for riveting, leathering and lining. An apprentice trained in the workshop for several years before qualifying as an armorer.

This 15th-century French royal helmet is gilded, embossed and enameled.

To make a sallet, a cold flat sheet was hammered down around the edges.

Hammering made the metal hard. They heated the metal to soften it.

The brim was beaten out and the edges turned over wire.

The polished helmet was fitted with a lining and chin strap.

Decoration

There was a whole team of people involved in making armor – armorers, finishers, polishers – and painters, etchers and gilders who decorated the armor. Some plate armor was painted, or colored blue by heating. The main edges might be decorated with borders of copper, latten (a kind of brass), or a precious metal such as silver or gold. Sometimes designs were engraved on these borders with a sharp point. By 1450 some designs were etched in with acid, and occasionally decorated with gold.

Horses

A knight was recognized by his horse – it was his distinguishing mark. Several European words for a knight actually mean 'horseman'. The knight's warhorse was a stallion, an aggressive animal that was specially bred and probably trained to bite and kick at opponents. It had a stout body with large lungs for staying power, and good muscles to carry an armored man. The high-backed saddle and long stirrups meant that the knight was almost welded to his horse – he was extremely secure, really almost standing upright. His horse was nimble and much smaller than a modern carthorse. In later centuries, knights owned more than one warhorse, in case one was killed, injured or too sick to be used. These horses were known as destriers, from the Latin for 'right', possibly because they were led on the right hand. A knight needed to be wealthy because a warhorse was extremely expensive to buy and to feed – each horse cost about as much as owning a car today. A lady might ride a gentle, smaller horse called a jennet. Ladies usually rode side-saddle, or in a litter slung between two horses. If a lady was the wife of a knight, he had to pay for her horses, too.

By the 13th century horses often wore a cloth covering called a trapper, bard or caparison. These might be padded, or made of mail (above). Some horses also wore a shaffron, or head-defense, made of leather or steel. Some shaffrons were painted.

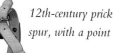

12th-century prick spur, with a point

15th-century rowel spur, with a wheel

Horses for All

The number of horses that a well-equipped knight needed meant that only wealthy men of rank could afford to become knights. The late 14th-century knight on the right is shown with four horses -the smallest number of mounts that was necessary. Often several retainers would need mounts, and extra riding or packhorses were required as well.

The destrier or courser, sometimes called the 'Great Horse', was the best and biggest of the knight's horses.

When not actually fighting, the knight rode a well-bred, easy-paced horse called a palfrey.

shaffron

crinet

peytral

Horse Armor

This late fifteenth century German armor covers most of the horse's body. Although full armor was available in the fourteenth century, most knights could afford armor only for the head, or perhaps the head, neck and chest. However well protected, there was usually a vulnerable part for an archer or foot soldier to aim at, such as the legs and belly.

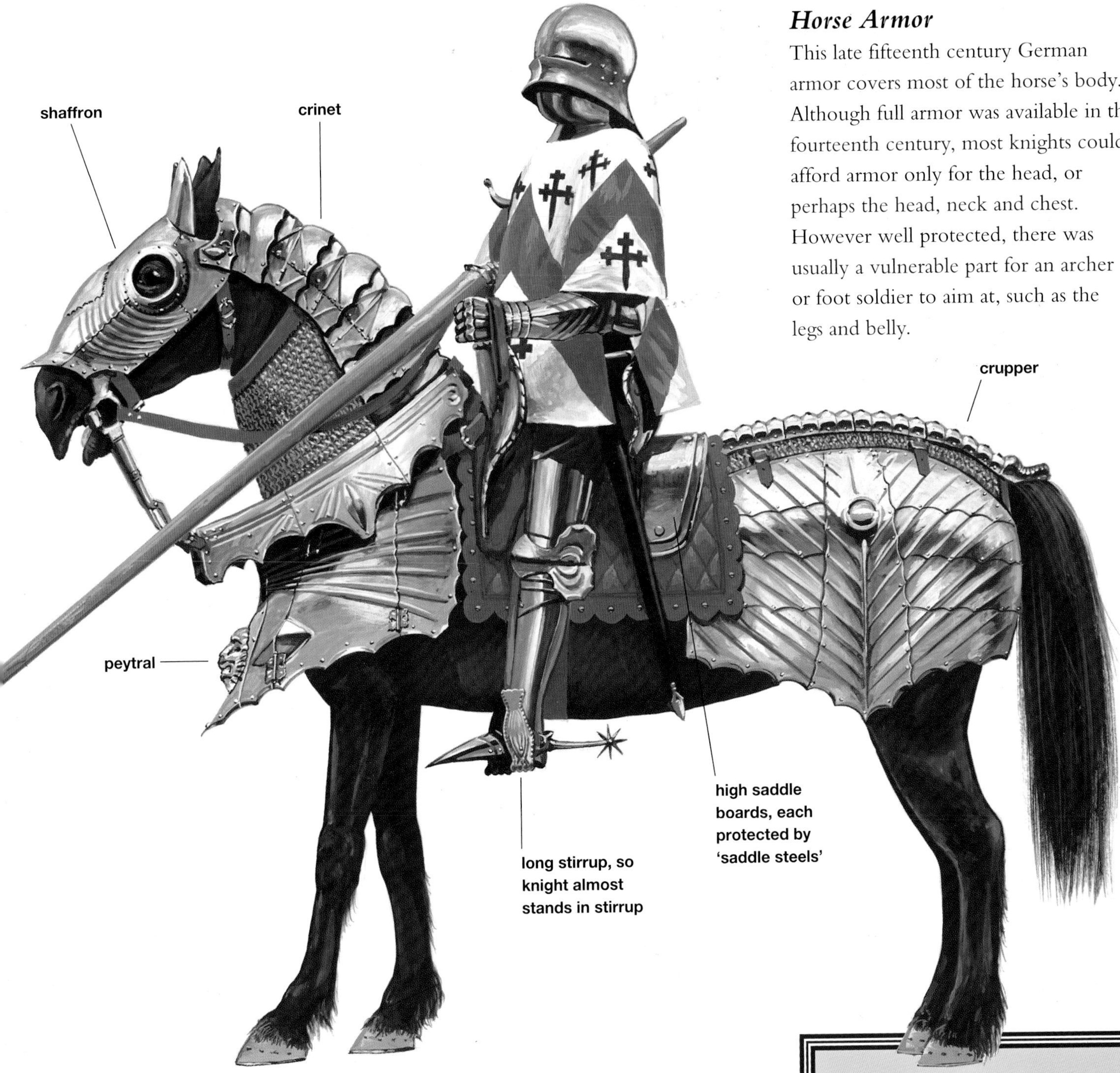

crupper

high saddle boards, each protected by 'saddle steels'

long stirrup, so knight almost stands in stirrup

Squires and retainers rode strong but less-well bred horses called rounceys; or, for the lesser servants, hackneys.

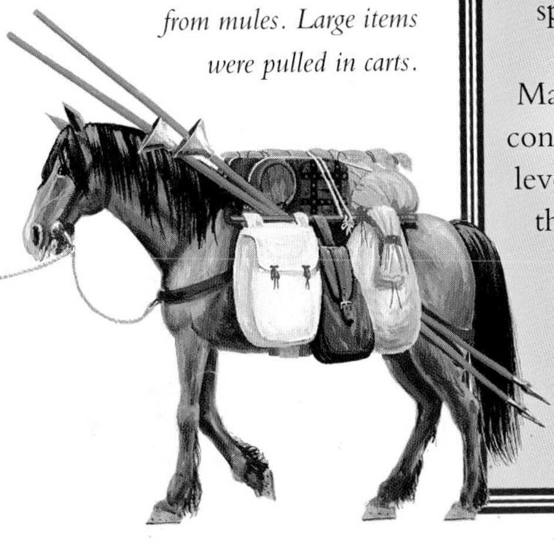

Baggage was carried in containers slung from packhorses/sumpters, or from mules. Large items were pulled in carts.

Horse facts

✷

By the 14th century, most knights wore spurs with a revolving spiked disc, called the rowel.

✷

Many knights used a curb bit to control their horse. This had long levers from the horse's mouth to the rein, which allowed great pressure to be applied.

✷

The weight of the horse armor shown above was 66lbs or 30 kg.

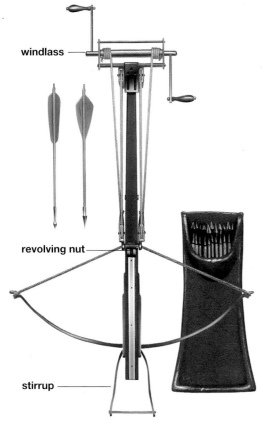

RETAINERS

A knight rarely acted alone. As well as his squires and pages, he might lead a group of armed followers, or retainers. This small group varied in size from century to century, and from place to place. In England, the knight and his retainers became known as a lance. A knight banneret was the leader of several lances. He carried a square or rectangular flag with his own heraldic arms. Several bannerets formed a battle, or division in the army. The lance shown below is based on a description in documents dating 1471-73 belonging to Charles the Bold, Duke of Burgundy. The knight wears full armor, with the red cross badge of Burgundy, and the plumes on his helmet and horse. He is attended by a mounted page. Also riding one of the knight's horses is a swordsman carrying a spear, a sword and a dagger. There are three mounted archers, each with 30 arrows, a two-hand sword and a dagger. On foot are a crossbowman, a handgunner and a pikeman.

This 15th-century crossbow has a powerful steel bow. The archer drew back the cord over a revolving nut by putting his foot in the stirrup and winding back the windlass. Crossbows shot short thick arrows called bolts. Early wooden bows were replaced with bows of wood, horn and sinew that needed various devices to draw them.

The mounted archers and crossbowman of this Burgundian lance wear brigandines, coats lined inside with small steel plates.

windlass

revolving nut

stirrup

36

Archers

The longbow was used in England in the late twelfth century, and possibly even before then. Unlike earlier bows, the bowman could draw it to his ear, sending an arrow a distance of over 300 yards. By the early fourteenth century, English and Welsh bowmen were greatly feared. The longbow, tall as a man, was often made of yew, and the arrows were usually fletched, or fitted with goose feathers. Many crossbows were drawn by special mechanisms and the cord was locked in place. But for every bolt shot by a crossbow, an archer could shoot up to 12 arrows. This archer wears a brigandine with mail sleeves and skirt.

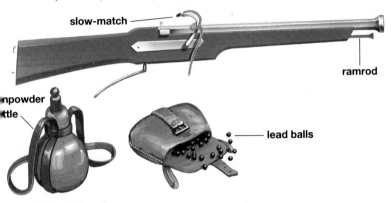

slow-match

ramrod

gunpowder bottle

lead balls

The Handgun

Handguns were introduced during the fourteenth century and became common in the fifteenth century. This late fifteenth-century example has an iron barrel into which a charge of gunpowder was poured. This was pushed down with a metal ramrod. A lead ball was then pushed in and a cloth wad was rammed in last. A hot wire or glowing slow-match, set against the touch-hole at the top, set off the charge.

Arrowheads varied, from needle-like bodkins for punching through armor (second down), to broadheads for maiming horses (third down).

37

IEGE WARFARE

When an invader wanted to capture a castle, he laid siege to it. The besieging army set up camp outside the walls to stop anyone from leaving, and to prevent supplies being taken in. If there was plenty of warning of an attack, the defenders got in with provisions and sometimes allowed local villagers to shelter within the walls. Some attackers were so feared that the defenders surrendered immediately. If they decided to hold out until help arrived, the besiegers surrounded the castle and settled down to starve out the inhabitants. Sometimes captives were tortured or executed in front of the castle to persuade the defenders to give in. If this did not work, a direct attack usually produced quicker results. This might involve launching an assault over the battlements, mining under the walls or using siege engines to smash holes in them. Once inside, the victorious besiegers slaughtered the defenders and looted the castle. Sieges were costly in time, men and money; but if an invader did not besiege castles as he advanced, the occupants might cut off his supply lines.

The trebuchet was a catapult that worked like a see-saw. When the short end of the arm was pulled down, the sling on the longer end flung a missile into the air. The traction trebuchet seen above is the earliest type. The short end was hauled down by a group of men pulling on ropes.

38

Trebuchet
The counterweight trebuchet had great weights to pull down the arm, and a long sling that could fling missiles over walls to shatter roofs.

Ballista
The giant crossbow could skewer men with its huge arrows. Some ballistas had two separate arms, each worked by a band of sinew.

Mangon
This catapult had an upright arm thrust through a thick band of twisted cords, or sinew. It hurled missiles against walls or timber hoardings.

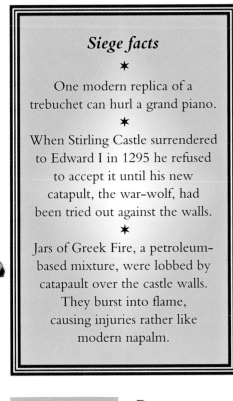
Mines and Siege Engines

Mines under the castle walls were
deadly. The defenders could detect the
miners by placing bowls of water on the
ground and watching for ripples. They
dug countermines so that they could
break into the mineshaft and destroy
the attackers' work. A wet moat, a ditch
with water in it, was a good defense
against mines. Sometimes the attackers
built a causeway over a dry ditch so
that their siege tower and battering ram
could be wheeled right up to the castle
walls. The defenders tried to deaden
the blows of the battering ram with
mattresses, or catch the head of the
ram with a grappling hook.

Defenders

*The defenders climbed onto
the wooden hoardings to
drop boulders, quicklime,
hot pitch, scalding water
or hot sand
onto attackers
who had
reached the
bottom of
the walls.*

Siege tower

*Towers called belfries
were dragged up to
the walls so that the
defenders could be
watched or picked off
by archers. Some
had a drawbridge
to allow the
attackers to
get onto the
battlements.*

Battering ram

*A huge tree trunk with an
iron head was swung at
the walls to crack them.*

Filling the Ditch

*The attackers made a causeway of
earth, rocks, rubble or refuse across
the dry ditch. This work was
carried out underneath wheeled
sheds so that the defenders could
not see what was going on.*

Mining

*The attackers dug mines under the
castle walls, supporting the roof with
timber props. Then they set fire to the
timber so that the props and the walls
above collapsed.*

BATTLE

Battles were extremely risky affairs because a king might lose his kingdom. Invading commanders often preferred to seize or burn an enemy lord's crops and to kill his peasants. This destroyed the lord's food supply and showed what poor protection he provided for his people. A lord might well shadow the enemy and prevent him from sending out troops, which also stopped him stealing food to feed his own men. If a battle was necessary, commanders looked for woods, bushes or rivers to guard their men. Knights owed allegiance and fought for the lord who kept them or who gave them land. From the fourteenth century, they often negotiated contracts for their service. Some knights and other soldiers were mercenaries, fighting for whoever paid them. Armies also included archers, crossbowmen, spearmen and eventually handgunners. In the picture below the knights 'couch', or level, their lances as they spur to a gallop on nearing the enemy, so as not to lose formation. They rode almost knee to knee, advancing like a steamroller.

The 15th-century rectangular banner of the Duke of Bourbon shows that he is a knight banneret, in command of other knights. It bears his heraldic arms and marks his position on the battlefield. His long standard shows his badges and motto: Esperance, meaning 'hope'. Mottoes were also used as battle-cries.

By the 14th century solid ranks of spearmen, or pikemen, were increasingly common. The Scotsman Robert the Bruce used them at Bannockburn in 1314 to stop the English knights. Only arrows could break their line. The Swiss became famous for their use, and they were copied by the Germans. The pikemen shown above are from the late 15th century.

The Battle of Agincourt, 1415

King Henry V of England was blocked near Agincourt during a large-scale raid. He positioned his army, five-sixths of which were archers, between two woods and went into attack. The French cavalry, hemmed in by trees, were shot down as they charged the archers. The French columns of dismounted men-at-arms became so jammed together that many suffocated.

Key

☑ French cavalry (mounted men-at-arms)
▪ French dismounted men-at-arms
▪ French archers and crossbowmen
▪ English dismounted men-at-arms
▪ English archers

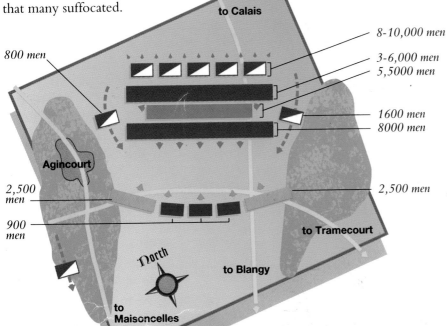

to Calais

800 men

8-10,000 men

3-6,000 men

5,5000 men

1600 men

8000 men

Agincourt

2,500 men

2,500 men

900 men

to Tramecourt

North

to Blangy

to Maisoncelles

Knights and Longbows

By the fourteenth century, English armies often combined large numbers of longbowmen with dismounted knights. The rate of fire from the longbows, up to 15 a minute, could kill or wound the horses of mounted men-at-arms, and demoralize any attacks launched on foot. From a good defensive position, the armies waited for the enemy to attack. Sometimes the archers carried sharp stakes to form a hedge of points. On the continent, crossbows were much more popular than in England.

 Tournament

The tournament probably started in the eleventh century, to provide training for battle. Two teams of knights armed with lances charged each other across a large area, often between two villages. When their lances broke, the knights continued with swords until sunset. Rest areas were provided for knights who needed a break, or they shielded themselves behind foot soldiers. There was little chivalry in a tournament. Knights ganged up on other knights and prisoners were taken. Defeated knights were forced to give up their horses and armor, or pay a ransom. This team event continued with little change until the thirteenth century, when blunted weapons slowly became popular and the combat area, or lists, grew smaller, making it easier to judge contests. More and more knights started to take part in individual contests with lances, called jousts; but the team event, the tourney, remained a great spectacle. In less formal contests called behourts, blunt weapons, such as whalebone swords, were always used and knights often wore lighter armor. In areas such as Germany, Hainalt, Flanders and parts of France, club tournaments were held in the fifteenth century. In these tournaments only the baston, a type of club, and blunt swords were used.

In the club tournament a knight wore a barred helmet, which was sometimes made of hardened leather. He attached his leather crest and cloth mantling on the spike at the top.

The knight often wore pierced armor to allow ventilation and to make the armor lighter. The lines down these leather arm-pieces were sticks, which were sometimes put in for extra reinforcement.

The blunted sword (top) and the club (below) were the only weapons used in the club tournament.

Pageantry and Ceremony

Tournaments took different forms and were always being held. One tournament in 1449 lasted for a year, with only four challenges a month being permitted. The Pas d'Armes of the fifteenth century was a spectacular form of tournament. A knight, or a group of knights, undertook to hold a piece of ground against all comers. At the Pass of the Shepherdess in 1446, real sheep were held in the arena. A tree of chivalry - either real or artificial - was symbolic and was used in many tournaments. The tree was either hung with the shields of those taking part, or, as shown here, colored shields represented forms of combat, such as the tourney, jousts and foot combat.
Those accepting the challenge, the 'answerers', or their heralds, touched the appropriate shield to select the form of combat. Rules set out the number of blows allowed. The lists measured anything from 100 by 80 yards up to 300 by 100 yards - 6 times the area of a football field. Stands were erected for nobles, ladies and judges. Kings and nobles, who originally saw tournaments as dangerous gatherings of fighting men, showed off by holding elaborate events.

The Church eventually gave up trying to ban them, especially as there were fewer fatalities.

43

In this tourney of about 1495 the knights wear reinforcing pieces which had to be removed as soon as a lance broke. Attendants stand within the double barrier to help their knight if he falls or is wounded.

JOUSTING

By 1250 a new form of combat in the tournament was becoming very popular. This was the joust, in which two mounted knights with lances charged each other. In the early days, all knights used lances with sharp points, just as they did in battle. Such jousts became known as 'jousts of war', the idea being for the jouster to test his skill and courage by knocking his opponent off his horse. But he didn't try to kill his opponent. It was only in the judicial duel that knights might fight to the death to settle matters of honor. Nevertheless, jousts of war were very dangerous and by 1250 another type of joust was increasingly seen. 'Jousts of peace' were so-called because blunted lances or ones fitted with a coronel were used. The main idea was for the jouster to break his own lance squarely against the other knight. Knights sometimes collided or missed because their horses did not run in a straight line, and so in the early fifteenth century a wooden barrier, the tilt, was introduced so that each knight could charge down one side. Some jousts, especially those of war, still used no barrier. Jousting was still popular after the medieval period, but in the seventeenth century it became rare. This coincided with armor disappearing from the battlefield.

Late 15th-century 'frog-mouthed' helm for jousts of peace.

44

'Frog-Mouthed' Helm

The 'frog-mouthed' jousting helm allowed the knight to see only when he leant forward. Straightening up before impact protected his eyes from his opponent's lance. The laces held a padded cap inside very tightly, to act as a shock absorber. The helm was often elaborately decorated.

Shield

The thick wooden shield for the armor on the left has two holes so that it could be tied through holes in the breastplate. The surface would often be painted or covered in cloth.

polder-mitten to guide blows away from elbow

queue to support butt (end) of lance

bare hand would be protected by lance vamplate

lance-rest to stop lance being pushed back

besagew

charnel

manifer

Aiming points

Mishaps

Before the tilt (barrier) came into use, knights could break their knees by passing too closely. In 1467 Lord Stanley was accused of using spiked horse armor when his opponent's horse collapsed after hitting his own. Despite safer helmets, two knights had their visors pierced at a tournament at Arras in 1430.

For jousts of war, knights often wore armor that was not very different from that used in real battle. For jousts of peace, special armor appeared which was reinforced especially on the left side because opponents passed each other on that side. For extra safety it was more rigid and of thicker steel than war armor, but only needed to be worn for short periods. The German armor on the left, dated about 1500, has no defenses for the legs as they were protected by side pieces on the saddle. The 'frog-mouthed' helm is stapled down to the breast and back-plates to prevent the head being hurled back by a lance-strike. The manifer guards the knight's hand and forearm.

45

lance

vamplate

coronel

FOOT COMBAT

A knight who was unhorsed during a joust occasionally agreed to carry on. His opponent also dismounted and both knights then fought on with their swords. On the battlefield, too, knights were increasingly fighting dismounted. By 1350 foot combat had become an event in its own right, usually forming part of a tournament. It normally took place between two contestants, who might be either knights or squires. For the contest the arena was surrounded by strong wooden barriers and the ground was thickly covered with sand. You might think that strength was the best ingredient for victory, but we are told that skill and speed were much more important. One fifteenth-century fighter leaped in the air when he entered the arena to demonstrate that his armor did not slow him in any way. He hoped to put off his opponent. The foot combat was a competition – it was not the same thing as a judicial combat held within barriers, when men fought to the death to settle a dispute.

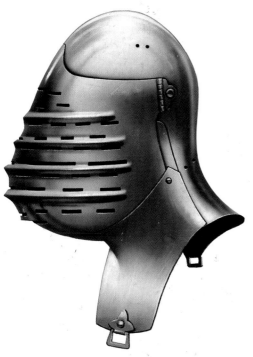

This fifteenth-century great basinet was originally used in battle, but because the plate neck and throat defenses made turning the head difficult, it gradually fell out of use. For foot combat in the tournament, however, where the fighting was much more orderly, knights welcomed the greater protection.

46

Jouarts, foot combat and tourneys were usually initiated by letters of challenge between knights. Here Lord Scales' herald delivers letters to the Bastard of Burgundy in 1465. A knight sometimes undertook to wear a certain item, such as a garter or piece of armor, until someone took up his challenge and fought him. Sometimes he had to actually win the contest before he could remove the item.

This late 15th-century Italian armor was a type specially made for foot combat. The great basinet with 'bellows' visor and the deep skirt, or tonlet, are typical features. No lance-rest is needed, so the knight's right shoulder-defense, or pauldron, is not cut away for his lance.

The pollaxe was a favorite weapon, though it could cause severe injury.

Fighting Within Barriers

Foot combat often began by each man throwing a spear, so at the start of a contest a knight might carry a shield at his left shoulder. As soon as the spears were thrown, the knights usually threw the shields aside because they were too much of a hindrance. The contestants here are attacking each other with pollaxes. All sorts of other weapons were also used: swords, daggers, axes, flails, maces, halberds and pikes. The exact form of contest was agreed beforehand, right down to the number of blows that should be struck. The blows were carefully noted during the contest – each man giving a blow alternately while the other tried to ward it off. At the end of the contest a referee decided which knight had struck the most skillful blows. Men-at-arms were stationed in the arena, equipped with wooden staves to separate the two contestants if they got entangled. In one contest we are told that a herald carried a length of rope with seven knots each about 2 ½ feet apart. These represented the number of paces the fighters had to retire before continuing the action.

Spanish castles such as Coca (above) were often influenced by Moorish decoration. In the Holy Land crusaders strengthened Muslim or Byzantine fortresses, and liked their castles to be protected on three sides by mountain crags or by water.

CRUSADES

A crusade is a campaign to protect Christianity, or to recapture Christian land or property. The first great crusade was organized by Pope Urban II in 1095. The Emperor of Byzantium (the area that stretched from modern Istanbul to Greece) asked for help against the Muslim Turks. A great army set out from western Europe and finally captured Jerusalem in 1099. Crusader states were set up in the Holy Land, but many soldiers then returned home. The Muslims became more united and eventually recaptured Jerusalem. There were six more major crusades, but they all failed. Even if they had been successful, the Christians could not have held Jerusalem with the few men who stayed behind. By 1291 the Muslims had pushed the Europeans out completely. Crusades took place in other places too: in Spain to drive out the Muslim Moors; in eastern Europe against heathen peoples; and even in France against heretics – Catholics who did not worship as the Pope wished.

This 12th-century horse-archer wears a coat of lamellar – small metal strips laced together. His bow of horn, wood and sinew is recurved at the ends for extra power.

Muslim Armies

Muslim forces came from different parts of south-east Asia and at first they were not particularly united. Under the great chief Saladin they combined and became a real threat. The Muslims used mounted archers on fast horses as well as heavier cavalry, and foot soldiers. The western knights were shot down as they tried to get to grips with them, or lost their precious warhorses to arrows. The picture opposite shows Richard I at the Battle of Arsuf in 1191 during the Third Crusade. The King protected his knights behind a marching wall of spearmen with shields, while archers and crossbowmen picked off Saladin's horse-archers. Richard wanted to force the Muslims closer so that his cavalry could charge out and destroy them. Unfortunately the knights at the end of the line charged out before the trumpet signal. Though successful, Richard knew that keeping his supply lines open was a problem, and finally made a treaty with Saladin, who was renowned for his chivalry.

Crusade facts

✲

There were seven major Crusades, taking place between 1095 and 1270.

✲

The Children's Crusade of 1212 was made up of peasants, including many children, from northern Europe. They did not get further than Rome.

✲

The Fourth Crusade in 1204 attacked Christian Constantinople, causing so much damage that the city fell to the Turks in 1453.

Warrior Monks

These thirteenth-century knights are monks who were members of the three main military Orders. The middle figure is a Templar, named after the Holy Temple in Jerusalem. A Hospitaller is on the right, and a knight of the German Teutonic Order on the left. These Orders were set up during the twelfth century. After the Holy Land was lost in 1291, the powerful Templars were abolished but the Hospitallers fought on in the Mediterranean area, while the Teutonic knights concentrated on fighting heathens in Eastern Europe.

HUNTING

Hunting provided meat for the dinner table, and was also a favorite sport. It gave the knights an opportunity to exercise their horses and to practice their riding skills. Most knights kept special horses for hunting, and for some the hunt was almost an obsession. For many knights, it was the only time they used a bow. Specially trained hunting dogs were sent out early in the morning to sniff out and track down prey. The knights chased game animals on horseback, or lay in wait with their bows while men beat the bushes and made noises to drive the animals towards them. William the Conqueror set aside vast areas of forest for his own private use. Foresters tended the woods and protected the animals chosen for hunting. Peasants who were caught poaching royal animals were severely punished. They might lose a hand, or even be executed. Dogs owned by the villagers who lived in these areas had their front claws cut off to stop them chasing game. Even nobles had to seek permission to hunt if the king's hunting ground included part of their own land.

The type of bird you hunted with depended on your rank in society. One early 15th-century lady wrote that the knight should have a saker falcon and the squire a lanner falcon. Here the falconer wears a leather glove to protect his hand from sharp claws. Thongs, called jesses, are attached to the bird's leg to stop it flying away. The hood keeps it calm and is taken off before release.

boar spear

broadhead

blunt

The boar spear had lugs to stop the animal sliding up the spear. The broadhead had long barbs, which gave a long cutting edge and stopped the broadhead falling out. The blunt was used to stun birds.

A wild boar is dangerous when angry. It was therefore quite a challenge for a knight to attack a boar on foot, using a boar spear. Here a powerful hunting dog called an alaunt is bringing the boar to bay. It wears an armored coat to protect it from sharp tusks.

Here a hunter is hiding behind a stalking-horse, a framework covered in dyed cloth. This could be used for stalking prey when there was no other cover.

A Hunting Party

In the picture below, noble lords and ladies of the early fifteenth-century ride out to fly their falcons. Falconry was a more gracious form of hunting than the chase on horseback. Some people kept their favorite bird in their chamber, but most birds of prey were kept in a long wooden shed called a mews.

The lymer (top) was a scenting hound for tracking game. The greyhound (center) was used for the chase. The spaniel was used when hunting birds

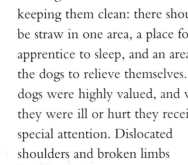

A Fifteenth-Century Kennel

Hunting dogs were kept in kennels in the castle courtyard. An old hunting book has instructions for keeping them clean: there should be straw in one area, a place for an apprentice to sleep, and an area for the dogs to relieve themselves. The dogs were highly valued, and when they were ill or hurt they received special attention. Dislocated shoulders and broken limbs were treated by bonesetters.

This pig in foil and individual heraldic pies were served to nobles at a 15th-century feast in Burgundy. Dinner did not consist of a meat course followed by a dessert - sweet and savory dishes arrived together. The names of some dishes were different too. Custard was a 'coffin' or pastry case filled with meat, herbs, dates, ginger, vinegar and eggs. Blancmange was a sort of meat or fish pie. Food was highly colored, and some cooked animals or birds stitched back in their skins to look alive.

The castle kitchen hummed with activity and was very hot, because food was cooked on an open fire. The boy turning the long pole on which a whole carcass is roasting was called a turnspit.

FOOD AND BANQUETS

In a medieval castle, mealtimes were different from those of today. For breakfast there was bread, washed down with ale or watered wine. Dinner, the main meal, was eaten at about ten or eleven in the morning, and supper between four and six o'clock. Some people also took another meal later on, accompanied by a great deal of drinking that sometimes continued until daybreak. The fourteenth-century banquet shown here marks an important event. On special occasions everyone ate together. There was a lot of food, drink and entertainment, because hospitality was admired. The lord, lady and guests sat at the high table set on a platform, the dais. Only those of great rank had chairs; everyone else had stools or benches. Most tables were on trestles so that they could be cleared away to make room for sleeping. Pages brought ewers, basins and napkins to wash the hands of the rich, while less important people used metal basins placed near the door. Everyone carried a personal knife, but forks were rare. Large slices of bread, or trenchers, were used as plates. These soaked up gravy, and any leftovers were given to the poor at the castle gate. Only the rich had actual plates made of pewter, silver or gold, and they did not share their food with anyone else. Roast meat was carved straight onto the trencher and people dipped the meat into saucers containing sauce. Bowls of thick meat stew were shared between two, each person fishing the meat out with his fingers. Thinner stews, sometimes made of fish, were also shared, but spoons were used. Even goblets of wine and beer could be shared between two. The castle being proudly carried in the picture is a 'subtlety', a sugar and marzipan model made by the cook. However, sugar was expensive, so honey and fruit were often used instead.

A FOURTEENTH·CENTURY·BANQUET

First course:
Brawn(pork); boar's head with trimmings; cygnets; capon; pheasant; heron. A subtlety.

Second course:
Venison; jelly (probably calf's foot); peacocks; cranes; bittern; fried brawn; tarts of several kinds. A subtlety.

Third course:
Quinces; egrets; curlews; partridges; quails; snipe; small birds; rabbits; fritters; iced eggs. A subtlety.

CHIVALRY

There was more to being a knight than just fighting and hunting – there was also chivalry. The word comes from an old French word for 'horse', but it came to mean a code of conduct that knights were supposed to follow. Books of chivalry advised knights to protect the weak, defend the church and fight for women. The earliest knights were rough fighting men and a favorite entertainment was the epic poem, an exciting tale of valor with plenty of fighting but little room for romance. During the twelfth century this began to change. The Church wanted to limit bloodshed by banning fighting on certain days, and it opposed the violence and deaths of the tournament. This opposition did not have much effect, but the Church gradually took more part in the creation of a knight. A new knight's sword was laid on the altar to be blessed and the knight agreed to defend the Church. Meanwhile, in southern France, minstrels, known as troubadours, were composing love songs for noble ladies at the courts. By the thirteenth century romance poems included deeds of courage, magic, and the rescue and love of ladies. The most famous were the stories of King Arthur and his Knights of the Round Table. The knight now had great examples to follow.

This 14th-century knight is dressed in the robes of the Order of the Garter, one of the earliest orders of chivalry, founded by Edward III of England in 1348. An order was a sort of club, and knights were proud to be chosen as members.

54

The Song of Roland is one of the most famous epic poems. It tells how Roland, commanding the rearguard in Emperor Charlemagne's army, returned to France over the Pyrenees in AD 775. He was attacked by the local Basque people and by Muslims at the pass at Roncesvalles, and the rearguard was almost wiped out. This picture shows Roland after he has failed to destroy his sword to stop the enemy taking it.

Knights of the Round Table

Arthur was probably a leader of the Britons in their wars against the Saxons in the sixth century, but medieval men thought of him as a knight of their own time. Stories about King Arthur, Queen Guinevere, Lancelot, the greatest knight, and the court at Camelot became themes for tournaments and also for social gatherings called 'Round Tables'. Here the Holy Grail, the cup used at the Last Supper of Christ, appears at the Round Table. The quest for the Grail was fulfilled by Galahad, the purest knight of all.

55

Chivalry facts

✱

The Court of Love was a light-hearted court held in Provence, France, in the twelfth century to sort out problems of love. Often run by ladies, it might decide which man was the real love of a particular lady.

✱

Sparing a knight in battle might be seen as chivalry, but often it was so that a ransom could be collected.

✱

Today a knighthood is a high honor conferred by the sovereign. It is a reward for service to one's country.

✱

The Court of Chivalry, which appeared in the 13th and 14th centuries, judged disputes between knights, including disagreements about who had the right to wear particular coats of arms.

A Knight does Homage to his Lady

Troubadours sang of their love for ladies who were impossible to win. These songs pleased the ladies at the court of Queen Eleanor of Aquitaine in southern France, and the songs spread throughout western Europe. Knights idolized ladies who they could never marry. This was part of the ritual of courtly love. Here a knight kneels before a lady who clasps his hands in imitation of the act of homage, where a man swore to serve his lord. Good manners and courtesy were marks of the accomplished knight.

LADIES

A knight usually wanted to marry – not necessarily for love, but because he was interested in an heiress, who would one day inherit her father's lands. Some ladies were widows and already owned estates. At the very least, a knight hoped for a wife with a large dowry, or wedding gift, from her father. Marriages were sometimes arranged when the bride was only a few years old. Death by accident and from disease was common, so a lady might have several husbands during her lifetime. Some couples did love each other and a wife was often a great help to her husband. While he went to war, or sat in court or parliament, she looked after the running of the castle and the estates.

Board games such as chess, checkers and backgammon were played by both men and women. Chess had slightly different rules to the modern game.

Ladies rode side-saddle or pillion on a saddle behind a man. Sometimes they traveled in a litter strung between two horses. This richly-decorated chair of the mid-14th century was used for ceremonial occasions. Riding in carts was otherwise rare, since condemned men rode that way to the gallows.

Sometimes a lady actually defended the castle during a siege. In peacetime she kept a check on the stores, ordered food and drink, bought cloth and other household items, and visited the farms. The lady approved the menus for daily meals, and also for feast days. She was expected to be the perfect hostess, greeting visitors and being on hand to bid them farewell.

Duties and Pastimes

The picture below shows how early fourteenth-century ladies spent their time. Ladies in the window seat are finishing an embroidery. Others are absorbed in dressmaking. A seamstress checks the cut of a half-finished dress, for fashionable clothes were as important then as now. Another pastime was spinning: the lady on the opposite page is using a distaff to draw out woolen thread. A servant combs out, or cards, more wool to get rid of impurities, for there were no machines to make wool. Some noblewomen were highly educated and could speak and read Latin and other languages. Some also wrote books. It was the duty of noblewomen to train young girls sent from other knightly households. While squires trained to be knights, young ladies were taught how to behave in polite society. Ladies-in-waiting were usually the wives and daughters of lesser knights who lived at the castle. Below them were a host of serving women. Wet nurses fed small babies at the breast, but nurses fed infants by chewing food before passing it to them. Washerwomen cleaned the castle clothing.

Like the knights, most ladies enjoyed hunting and were excellent horsewomen. The thirteenth-century lady above carries a longbow. This was not as powerful as the bow used in battle, but it was strong enough to kill deer. Ladies could also use crossbows.

57

DECLINE

In the late fifteenth century, the Swiss and German landesknecht *signified the loss of influence of the knight. Their ranks of pikeman, backed by guns, set the form of warfare for the next 200 years. This German* landesknecht *carries a two-hand sword was for slashing a path through a line of enemy pikemen.*

By the early sixteenth century knights were losing their importance. More and more countries had organized professional armies, and the knight with his lance was no match for their ranks of pikemen. Nor did the knight's armor protect him against the handgunners. Armorers tried making thicker breastplates that were tested, or proofed, by firing a gun at them - rather like a bullet-proof vest today. Sometimes a second, reinforcing breastplate was strapped over the first one. But, not surprisingly, the knights refused to wear such heavy armor, or they left off leg-pieces to reduce the weight and wore boots instead. By the mid-seventeenth century the armored horseman was on his way out.

The knight's home, the castle, also suffered. This was partly because the knight demanded better comfort, but also because of the increased use of cannon. At first, openings for cannon were made in the existing castle walls. Then, starting in France and Italy, cannon were set on low, thick earth-filled bastions instead of high walls. These became the artillery forts of the sixteenth century and, in time, were no longer a knight's private home but a government garrison.

Rulers were building foundries to produce cannon for their armies, like this 16th-century one

Harquebusiers

These mid-seventeenth-century horsemen wore very little armor in comparison to the fully armored knight. They wore tough, buff leather coats, breastplates and elbow gauntlets on their left arms. Their helmets triple-barred visors to stop a sword slash. As well as swords, they carried pistols. Their odd-sounding name comes from the word 'arquebus', which was originally an early long-barreled matchlock gun but was later used to refer to their handguns.

THE KNIGHT'S WORLD

This map shows how extensive the world of the knight was. Areas where certain goods could be obtained are marked by the name of the item. The routes used by traders and by the crusaders have been simplified. Some of the most important centers for making armor are shown, but others also existed. A selection of major castles and the main centers for pilgrimages are included.

BANNOCKBURN

coal
cloth

fish

TOWTON

LÜBECK

CAERPHILLY CHEPSTOW corn
wool

tin

Tower of
London

LONDON

HASTINGS

BRUGES GHENT Antwerp COLOGNE
COURTRAI

AGINCOURT BRUSSELS iron MARKSBURG
copper

CHATEAU cloth lead COBURG
GAILLARD beer
silver AUSSIG

PATAY PARIS

corn NUREMBERG gold

ANGER wool AUGSBURG LANDSHUT
salt wine
TOURS cloth

LOCHES GRANDSON INNSBRUCK
SEMPACH

wool LYONS

wine MILAN CASTAGNARO
FORNOVO VENICE

SANTIAGO DE GENOA
COMPOSTELA

BURGOS CARCASSONNE MARSEILLES FLORENCE

LISBON

SAGRAJAS wool ROME
wine
mercury
sugar VALENCIA

SEVILLE LAS NAVAS DE TOLOSA

GRANADA

TUNIS

FEZ

sugar
fruit

gold
ivory
slaves

Key

- ········· Trade routes
- – – – Eastern crusades
- ⠿⠿⠿⠿ Spanish and Baltic crusades
- Armor-making centers
- Castles
- ✕ Battles
- ✚ Major centers of pilgrimage

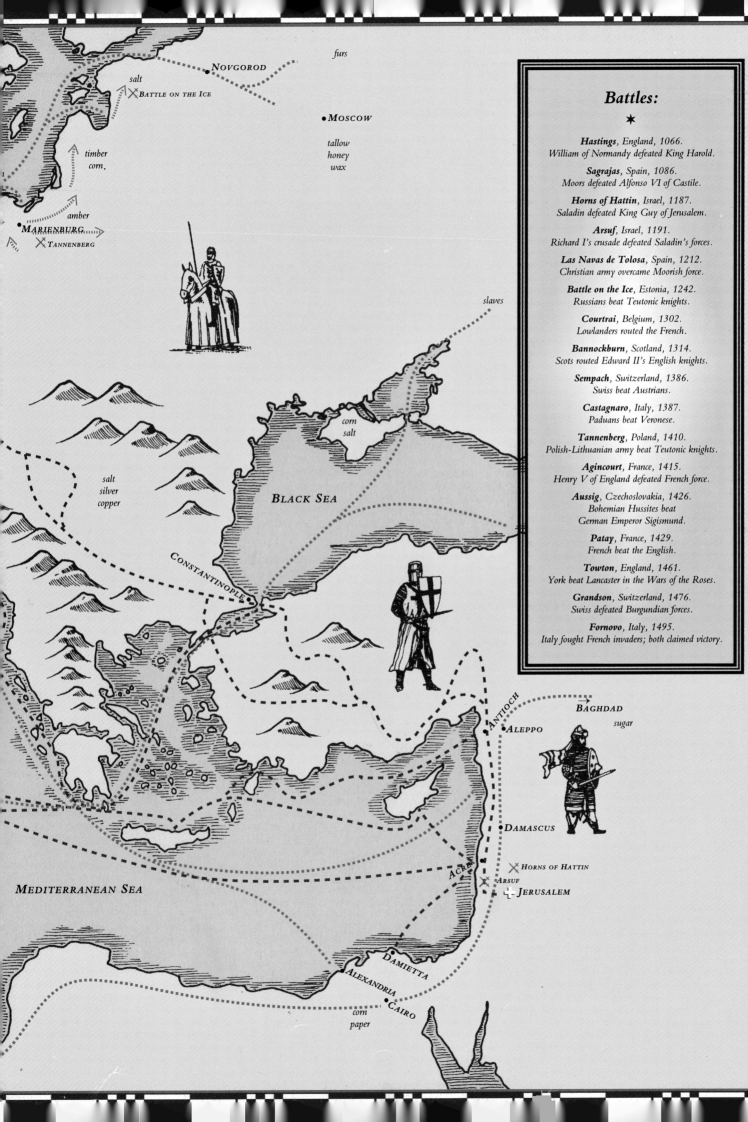

furs

NOVGOROD

salt

×BATTLE ON THE ICE

•MOSCOW

tallow
honey
wax

timber
corn.

amber

•MARIENBURG
×TANNENBERG

slaves

timber
corn

salt
silver
copper

corn
salt

BLACK SEA

CONSTANTINOPLE

ANTIOCH

BAGHDAD

•ALEPPO

sugar

DAMASCUS

MEDITERRANEAN SEA

ACRE

×HORNS OF HATTIN

×ARSUF

✝JERUSALEM

DAMIETTA

ALEXANDRIA

•CAIRO

corn
paper

61

Battles:

★

Hastings, England, 1066.
William of Normandy defeated King Harold.

Sagrajas, Spain, 1086.
Moors defeated Alfonso VI of Castile.

Horns of Hattin, Israel, 1187.
Saladin defeated King Guy of Jerusalem.

Arsuf, Israel, 1191.
Richard I's crusade defeated Saladin's forces.

Las Navas de Tolosa, Spain, 1212.
Christian army overcame Moorish force.

Battle on the Ice, Estonia, 1242.
Russians beat Teutonic knights.

Courtrai, Belgium, 1302.
Lowlanders routed the French.

Bannockburn, Scotland, 1314.
Scots routed Edward II's English knights.

Sempach, Switzerland, 1386.
Swiss beat Austrians.

Castagnaro, Italy, 1387.
Paduans beat Veronese.

Tannenberg, Poland, 1410.
Polish-Lithuanian army beat Teutonic knights.

Agincourt, France, 1415.
Henry V of England defeated French force.

Aussig, Czechoslovakia, 1426.
Bohemian Hussites beat
German Emperor Sigismund.

Patay, France, 1429.
French beat the English.

Towton, England, 1461.
York beat Lancaster in the Wars of the Roses.

Grandson, Switzerland, 1476.
Swiss defeated Burgundian forces.

Fornovo, Italy, 1495.
Italy fought French invaders; both claimed victory.

GLOSSARY

Alaunt
Powerful hunting dog.

Arming doublet
Doublet with mail attached and with fastenings for attaching armor.

Armet
Helmet that opens at the sides when put on.

Aketon
A padded tunic worn under mail and also on its own by less well-armed soldiers.

Aventail
Neck-defense of mail, attached to a bassinet or armet.

Ballista
Siege engine that shoots a large arrow.

Bailey
Castle courtyard.

Banner
Square or rectangular flag carried by a banneret, displaying his arms.

Banneret
A knight who commands other knights.

Bassinet
Type of helmet reaching or covering the ears, often worn with a visor.

Bodkin
Slender arrow-head for piercing armor.

Bolt
Short arrow for a crossbow.

Brigandine
Jacket lined with many small steel plates attached by rivets – the rivet heads show on the outside of the jacket.

Broadhead
Arrowhead with large cutting surface, ending in two barbs.

Butler
A lord's official in charge of the buttery.

Buttery
A store for bottles.

Cannon
Large gun fired from a support; also, a plate defense for the lower or upper arm.

Char
A large wheeled carriage for ladies.

Chausse
Mail stocking.

Coat of plates
Body armor of material lined, or occasionally faced, with a number of plates.

Cop
Small plate worn at the elbow or knee.

Courser
Fast horse, sometimes the war-horse.

Courtly love
A knightly code of behavior towards ladies. Knights had to prove their love towards a lady (who was often promised or married to another man) by performing heroic deeds and reciting love poems.

Couter
An elbow-defense.

Crinet
A horse's neck-defense.

Crupper
A horse's rump-defense.

Crusades
The Crusades were Christian military expeditions undertaken between 1095 and 1270 to seize the Holy Land from the Muslims. The word 'crusade' comes from the Latin, *crux*.

Cuirass
Defense for the breast and back.

Cuisse
Thigh-defense.

Curie
A leather defense for the breast and back.

Destrier
The great horse, or war-horse.

Donjon
Great tower, or keep.

Ewer
A type of jug for holding water.

Falchion
Short, single-edged cutting sword with a blade that is wider towards the point.

Flail
A weapon adapted from a farming tool for threshing. It consists of a handle to which is hinged a baton studded with spikes.

Fuller
Channel running down the center of a sword blade to reduce the weight.

Gauntlet
Armored glove.

Greave
Lower leg-defense.

Hackney
A rather poor riding horse.

Halberd
Weapon that is a combination of a spear and a battleaxe, consisting of a sharp-edged blade backed by a beak and ending in a point, and mounted on a long handle.

Hauberk
The French word for a mail coat, originally referring to a neck-guard only.

Helm
Type of helmet that completely covers the head.

Holy Land
The area in which Christ lived and worked – largely modern Israel.

Holy Temple
The ancient temple in Jerusalem in which Christ taught.

Jennet
A horse for a lady.

Jesses
Leather thongs fastened to the legs of a falcon or hawk to restrain it.

Joust
In a tournament, a combat between two mounted opponents armed with lances.

Judicial combat
A fight between two contestants to settle a matter of honor.

Keep
Stone tower, known as a great tower or donjon.

Kettle hat
Open helmet with a broad brim.

Lance
Wooden shaft fitted with a pointed steel head, for use on horseback.

Lance-rest
A fitting on the breast-plate that helps support the knight's lance and prevent it being pushed back on impact.

Lymer
Hound for scenting game.

Mace
Weapon with a solid iron or steel head, used for dealing crushing blows.

Mail
Armor made from inter-linked and riveted iron rings.

Mangon
Type of catapult that is operated using twisted rope, sinew or hair.

Manor
A piece of land owned by a lord, including his personal holding and those of his villagers.

Marshal
A lord's official in charge of military matters, horses etc.

Men-at-arms
Used in the 14th century to mean knights and squires; from the 15th century it included armored men below the rank of knights and squires.

Motte
An earth mound.

Orders
Special bands or clubs of knights with special uniforms and emblems. Each Order had a distinctive name, such as Order of the Poor Knights of Christ (or Knights Templars) or Knights of Saint John of Jerusalem (or Knights Hospitallers).

Palfrey
A good riding horse.

Pantry
A store for dry foods, such as bread and salt.

Pauldron
A shoulder-defense that overlaps the chest and back.

Pike
Very long spear used by foot soldiers.

Pilgrimage
A special journey to a holy place.

Point
Thong with a metal tip, for attaching clothing or armor.

Pollaxe
Long staff topped with a spiked axe-head or a hammer.

Poleyn
A knee-defense.

Pommel
The weight fitted over the end of a sword hilt.

Portcullis
An iron-studded wooden lattice that was dropped down to defend a castle gateway.

Prick spur
A spur fitted with a point.

Rouncey
An average riding horse.

Rowel spur
A spur fitted with a revolving star-shaped wheel, or rowel.

Sabaton
Foot-defense.

Schiltron
A dense mass of infantry armed with spears or pikes.

Schynbald
A shin-defense.

Sewer
Head waiter and also chief food taster of a lord. He checked whether food was poisoned.

Shaffron
A horse's head-defense.

Siege
An attack on a fortification.

Staff-weapon
A weapon mounted on a long wooden haft, or handle.

Standard
Long flag used by kings and nobles as a rallying point.

Steward
A lord's official in charge of the household.

Sumpter
A pack-horse or pack-mule.

Teutonic Knights
The full name was Teutonic Knights of Saint Mary's Hospital at Jerusalem. A religious military order formed by German Crusaders in 1190-91 in Acre.

Tithe
A tenth, the amount taken by the church as a tax.

Tournament
An event that included combats on horseback and sometimes on foot.

Tourney
In a tournament, a mounted combat between two teams armed with lances and swords or other weapons.

Trebuchet
Catapult with weights to pull down the arm, and a long sling that could fling missiles over castle walls.

Vambrace
Arm-defense.

Vamplate
Circular or conical steel disc fitted to a lance to guard the knight's hand.

Villein
An unfree peasant, tied to the land he worked on.

Visor
A face-guard, pierced with vision-slits and breathing holes.

Windlass
Pulley system for winding back the cord of crossbows.

INDEX

A

Agincourt, battle of 41, 61
aketon 20, 62
alaunt 50, 62
alwite 20
archers 8, 9, 35, 36, 37, 39, 40, 41, 49
arm defenses 22-3
armet 27, 29, 62
armor 14, 15, 16-29, 32-3, 35, 42, 44, 45, 47, 58, 60, 62, 63
armorer 16, 19, 21, 23, 28, 32, 33, 58
arrows 8, 16, 37, 41, 62
Arthur, King 54, 55
aventail 26, 62
axes 31, 47

B

bailey 8, 62
ballista 38, 62
banneret 36, 40, 62
banners 40, 62
banquets 52-3
basinet 17, 26, 27, 46, 47, 62
battering ram 9, 39
Battle of Hastings 27, 60, 61
battles 15, 40-1, 55, 60, 61
Bembre, Sir Nicholas 25
birds of prey 51
Black Death 12
Black Prince 24
boar 50
bodkin 37, 62
Bourbon, Duke of 40
bread ovens 13
breastplate 20, 21, 45, 58
brigandine 18, 36, 37, 62
Byzantium 48

C

Caerphilly Castle (Wales) 9
Camelot 55
cannons 58, 62
cap-a-pie 29
castles 7, 8-11, 13, 38-9, 48, 51, 52, 56, 57, 58, 60, 63
catapults 38, 39, 63
cavalry 41, 49
cervellière 26
chaisses 18
Charlemagne, Emperor 7, 54
Charles the Bold, Duke of Burgundy 36
chausses 62
Chepstow Castle (Wales) 10-11
children 14, 57
chivalry 7, 42, 43, 49, 54-5
Christianity 48, 49, 62
Church 7, 13, 43, 54
clubs 42
coat of plates 20, 62
Coca Castle (Spain) 48
concentric castles 9
Constantinople 49, 61
crossbows 36, 37, 38, 41, 49, 57, 62, 63
Crusades 48-9, 60, 62, 63
cuirass 20-1, 62
cuisses 18, 19, 28, 62

D

daggers 31, 47
destriers 34, 62
dogs 50, 51, 62, 63
donjons 8, 62, 63
doublets 28, 62
drawbridges 8, 39
dubbing 15

E

Edward I, King 39
Edward III, King 20, 54
El Cid 35
Eleanor of Aquitaine 55

F

falchion 30, 62
falconry 50, 51, 62
farms 12, 56
fauld 21, 29
flags 36, 62, 63
food 10, 11, 14, 40, 52-3, 56, 63
foot combat 43, 46-7
fortresses 8
France 7, 41, 42, 48, 54, 55, 58, 60, 61
Franks 7
'frog-mouthed' helm 44, 45

G

gadlings 24, 25
garrisons 8, 58
gatehouses 8, 9, 10
gauntlets 24-5, 58, 62
Germany 7, 16, 17, 21, 22, 25, 27, 31, 35, 41, 42, 45, 58, 60, 63
Gothic armor 21
Great Hall 10, 11, 53
greaves 18, 19, 28, 62
guns 37, 58

H

halberd 31, 47, 62
handguns 37, 58
harquebusiers 58
Hastings, Sir Hugh 22
hauberk 16, 20, 62
helm 17, 26, 44, 45, 62
helmets 16, 26-7, 29, 32, 33, 42, 45, 58, 63
Henry V, King 41, 61
heraldic arms 36, 40, 45, 55
heralds 43, 47
Holy Grail 55
Holy Land 48, 49, 62
horses 13, 14, 16, 17, 18, 30, 34-5, 41, 42, 44, 45, 49, 50, 56, 58, 62, 63
hose 28
Hospitallers 49, 63
houses 12, 13
hunting 14, 50-1, 57, 62

I

Italy 16, 17, 19, 21, 23, 25, 27, 28, 32, 47, 60, 61

J

Jerusalem 48, 49, 61, 62
Joan of Arc 18
jousts 42, 43, 44-5, 46, 47, 62
judical duel 44, 46, 63

K

keeps 8, 9, 62, 63
kennels 51
kettle hat 26, 63
kings 12, 13, 15, 24, 40, 43, 50, 63
kitchens 11, 52

L

ladies 7, 14, 34, 43, 45, 50, 51, 52, 54, 55, 56-7, 62
lances 15, 21, 23, 30, 36, 40, 42, 44, 45, 47, 58, 62, 63
leg armor 18-19
lists 42, 43
longbows 37, 41, 57
lords 10, 13, 14, 40, 51, 52, 63
Louis XI, King 28
love, courtly 54, 55, 62

M

maces 31, 47, 63
mail armor 15, 16, 17, 18, 19, 24, 28, 31, 32, 34, 37, 63
mangon 38, 63
manors 12-13, 63
marriage 13, 56
Marshal, William 27
men-at-arms 7, 41, 47, 63
mercenaries 7, 40
merchants 13
mines 38, 39
minstrels 54
moats 9, 39
monks 49
motte 8, 63
mottoes 40
mufflers 24
Muslims 13, 17, 48, 49, 54, 62

N

Nesle, Raoul de 25
nobles 7, 12, 43, 50, 51, 57

O

Order of the Garter 54
Orders 49, 54, 63
ordinances 36

P

pages 14, 28, 36, 52
palfrey 34, 63
palisades 7, 8
Pas d'Armes 43
pauldron 23, 29, 47, 63
peasants 12, 40, 49, 50, 63
pikemen 41, 58
pikes 47, 63
pilgrimages 60, 63
plate armor 16, 17, 18, 31, 33
poachers 12, 50
poems 54, 62
poleyn 18, 19, 28, 63
pollaxe 31, 47, 63
portcullis 8, 63

Q

quintain 15

R

ransoms 11, 42, 55
retainers 34, 35, 36-7
Richard I, King 49
Robert the Bruce 41
Rome 49, 60
'Round Table' 54, 55

S

sabaton 19, 63
saddles 34, 35, 45, 56
Saladin 49, 61
sallet 27, 33
scabbard 30
schynbald 18, 63
sentries 11
shields 16, 17, 22, 23, 43, 45, 47, 49
shoulder defenses 23
siege towers 39
sieges 10, 38-9, 56, 63
Spain 13, 48, 60, 61
spearmen 40, 41, 49
spears 47, 50, 63
spurs 15, 29, 34, 35, 63
squires 7, 14-15, 28, 29, 34, 35, 36, 46, 57, 63
staff weapons 31, 63
stalking-horse 51
standards 40, 63
Stirling Castle (Scotland) 39
stocks 12
surcoat 17, 20
Switzerland 31, 41, 58, 60, 61
swords 15, 16, 22, 24, 26, 29, 30, 31, 42, 46, 47, 54, 58, 62, 63

T

Templars 49, 63
Teutonic Knights 49, 61, 63
tilt 44, 45
tithe 12, 63
tournaments 17, 34, 42-7, 54, 62, 63
tourney 42, 43, 47
towers 8, 9, 63
towns 13
Towton, battle of 41
training 14-15, 42, 57
trebuchet 38, 39, 63
troubadours 54, 55

U

Urbán II, Pope 48

V

vambrace 22, 23, 63
vamplate 30, 45, 63
vigil 15
Vikings 7
villages 12-13, 42
visors 26, 31, 45, 47, 58, 63

W

war hammer 31
Warwick, Earl of 17
weapons 14, 15, 16, 22, 24, 25, 30-1, 36-7, 42, 47, 62, 63
William the Conqueror 27, 50, 61
wounds 18, 19, 22, 24, 30, 41